MY MEDITERRANEAN RECIPES

DELICIOUS AND EASY RECIPES FOR ANY OCCASION

FOR BEGINNERS

SAMANTHA GALLAGHER

Smoked Salmon Scrambled Egg

Preparation Time : 2 minutes

Cooking Time : 8 minutes

Servings : 4

Difficulty Level : Average

Ingredients:

- 16 ounces egg substitute, cholesterol-free
- 1/8 teaspoon of black pepper
- 2 tablespoons of sliced green onions, keep the tops
- 1 ounce of chilled reduced-fat cream cheese, cut into 1/4-inch cubes
- 2 ounces of flaked smoked salmon

Directions:

Cut the chilled cream cheese into ¼-inch cubes then set aside. Whisk the egg substitute and the pepper in a large sized bowl Coat a non-stick skillet with cooking spray over medium heat. Stir in the egg substitute and cook for 5 to 7 minutes or until it starts to set stirring occasionally and scraping bottom of the pan.

Fold in the cream cheese, green onions and the salmon. Continue to cook and stir for another 3 minutes or just until the eggs are still moist but cooked.

Nutrition (for 100g): 100 Calories 3g Fats 2g Carbohydrates 15g Protein 772mg Sodium

Hummus Deviled Egg

Preparation Time : 10 minutes

Cooking Time : 0 minutes

Servings : 6

Difficulty Level : Easy

Ingredients :

- 1/4 cup of finely diced cucumber
- 1/4 cup of finely diced tomato
- 2 teaspoons of fresh lemon juice
- 1/8 teaspoon salt
- 6 hard-cooked peeled eggs, sliced half lengthwise
- 1/3 cup of roasted garlic hummus or any hummus flavor
- Chopped fresh parsley (optional)

Directions:

Combine the tomato, lemon juice, cucumber and salt together and then gently mix. Scrape out the yolks from the halved eggs and store for later use. Scoop a heaping teaspoon of humus in each half egg. Top with parsley and half-teaspoon tomato-cucumber mixture. Serve immediately

Nutrition (for 100g): 40 Calories 1g Fat 3g Carbohydrates 4g

Directions:

Coat with a cooking spray a small size non-stick skillet. Stir in the onion and red pepper for 3 minutes over medium heat. Add your egg substitute and season with salt and pepper. Stir cook until it sets. Mix the torn spinach, chopped tomatoes, and mince basil. Scoop onto the pitas. Top vegetable mixture with your egg mixture. Topped with crumbled feta cheese and serve immediately.

Nutrition (for 100g): 267 Calories 3g Fat 41g Carbohydrates 20g Protein 643mg Sodium

Mediterranean Pita Breakfast

Preparation Time : 22 minutes

Cooking Time : 3 minutes

Servings : 2

Difficulty Level : Easy

Ingredients :

- 1/4 cup of sweet red pepper
- 1/4 cup of chopped onion
- 1 cup of egg substitute
- 1/8 teaspoon of salt
- 1/8 teaspoon of pepper
- 1 small chopped tomato
- 1/2 cup of fresh torn baby spinach
- 1-1/2 teaspoons of minced fresh basil
- 2 whole size pita breads
- 2 tablespoons of crumbled feta cheese

Greek Dinner Salad 171

Halibut with Lemon-Fennel Salad...173

Herbed Greek Chicken Salad 175

Greek Couscous Salad..177

Denver Fried Omelet 179

Sausage Pan..181

Grilled Marinated Shrimp 183

Sausage Egg Casserole 185

Baked Omelet Squares 187

Hard-Boiled Egg 189

Mushrooms with a Soy Sauce Glaze..190

Egg Cupcakes 192

Dinosaur Eggs 194

Paleo Almond Banana Pancakes..198

Zucchini with Egg 200

Cheesy Amish Breakfast Casserole 201

Salad with Roquefort Cheese 203

Rice with Vermicelli 205

Fava Beans and Rice 207

Buttered Fava Beans...209

Freekeh...210

Fried Rice Balls with Tomato Sauce..211

Spanish-Style Rice...213

Zucchini with Rice and Tzatziki 215

Cannellini Beans with Rosemary and Garlic Aioli 217

Jeweled Rice 218

Asparagus Risotto...220

Chicken Salad	128
Cobb Salad	130
Broccoli Salad	132
Strawberry Spinach Salad	134
Pear Salad with Roquefort Cheese	136
Mexican Bean Salad	138
Melon Salad	140
Orange Celery Salad	142
Roasted Broccoli Salad	143
Tomato Salad	145
Feta Beet Salad	146
Cauliflower & Tomato Salad	147
Pilaf with Cream Cheese	148
Roasted Eggplant Salad	150
Roasted Veggies	151
Pistachio Arugula Salad	153
Parmesan Barley Risotto	154
Seafood & Avocado Salad	156
Mediterranean Shrimp Salad	158
Chickpea Pasta Salad	159
Mediterranean Stir Fry	161
Balsamic Cucumber Salad	163
Beef Kefta Patties with Cucumber Salad	164
Chicken and Cucumber Salad with Parsley Pesto	166
Easy Arugula Salad	168
Feta Garbanzo Bean Salad	169
Greek Brown and Wild Rice Bowls	170

Brekky Egg- Potato Hash	82
Basil and Tomato Soup	84
Butternut Squash Hummus	86
Ham Muffins	87
Farro Salad	88
Cranberry and Dates Squares	89
Lentils and Cheddar Frittata	90
Tuna Sandwich	92
Spelled Salad	93
Chickpea and Zucchini Salad	95
Provencal Artichoke Salad	97
Bulgarian Salad	99
Falafel Salad Bowl	101
Easy Greek Salad	103
Arugula Salad with Figs and Walnuts	105
Cauliflower Salad with Tahini Vinaigrette	107
Mediterranean Potato Salad	109
Quinoa and Pistachio Salad	111
Cucumber Chicken Salad with Spicy Peanut Dressing	113
German Hot Potato Salad	114
Chicken Fiesta Salad	116
Corn & Black Bean Salad	118
Awesome Pasta Salad	119
Tuna Salad	121
Southern Potato Salad	122
Seven-Layer Salad	124
Kale, Quinoa & Avocado Salad with Lemon Dijon Vinaigrette	126

Mini Lettuce Wraps 48

Curry Apple Couscous 49

Lamb & Vegetable Bake 50

Herb Flounder 52

Cauliflower Quinoa 53

Mango Pear Smoothie 54

Spinach Omelet 55

Almond Pancakes 57

Quinoa Fruit Salad 59

Strawberry Rhubarb Smoothie 60

Barley Porridge 61

Gingerbread & Pumpkin Smoothie 62

Green Juice 63

Walnut & Date Smoothie 64

Fruit Smoothie 65

Chocolate Banana Smoothie 66

Yogurt with Blueberries, Honey, and Mint 67

Berry and Yogurt Parfait 68

Oatmeal with Berries and Sunflower Seeds 69

Almond and Maple Quick Grits 70

Banana Oats 72

Breakfast Sandwich 73

Morning Couscous 75

Avocado and Apple Smoothie 77

Mini Frittatas 78

Sun-dried Tomatoes Oatmeal 80

Breakfast Egg on Avocado 81

Table of Contents

Mediterranean Pita Breakfast 9

Hummus Deviled Egg 11

Buckwheat Apple-Raisin Muffin 13

Pumpkin Bran Muffin 15

Buckwheat Buttermilk Pancakes 17

French Toast with Almonds and Peach Compote 18

Mixed Berries Oatmeal with Sweet Vanilla Cream.............................. 20

Choco-Strawberry Crepe 22

No Crust Asparagus-Ham Quiche 24

Apple Cheese Scones 26

Bacon and Egg Wrap 28

Orange-Blueberry Muffin 30

14. Baked Ginger Oatmeal with Pear Topping 31

Greek Style Veggie Omelet... 32

Summer Smoothie 34

Ham & Egg Pitas... 35

Breakfast Couscous 37

Peach Breakfast Salad... 39

Savory Oats 40

Tahini & Apple Toast 41

Scrambled Basil Eggs 42

Greek Potatoes & Eggs 43

Avocado & Honey Smoothie.. 45

Vegetable Frittata.. 46

Buckwheat Apple-Raisin Muffin

Preparation Time : 24 minutes

Cooking Time : 20 minutes

Servings : 12

Difficulty Level : Average

Ingredients:

- 1 cup of all-purpose flour
- 3/4 cup of buckwheat flour
- 2 tablespoons of brown sugar
- 1 1/2 teaspoons of baking powder
- 1/4 teaspoon of baking soda
- 3/4 cup of reduced-fat buttermilk
- 2 tablespoons of olive oil
- 1 large egg
- 1 cup peeled and cored, fresh diced apples
- 1/4 cup of golden raisins

Directions:

Prepare the oven at 375 degrees F. Line a 12-cup muffin tin with a non-stick cooking spray or paper cups. Set aside. Incorporate all the dry ingredients in a mixing bowl. Set aside.

Beat together the liquid ingredients until smooth. Transfer the liquid mixture over the flour mixture and mix until moistened. Fold in the diced apples and raisins. Fill each muffin cups with about 2/3 full of the mixture. Bake until it turns golden brown. Use the toothpick test. Serve.

Nutrition (for 100g): 117 Calories 1g Fat 19g Carbohydrates 3g Protein 683mg Sodium

Pumpkin Bran Muffin

Preparation Time : 20 minutes
Cooking Time : 20 minutes
Servings : 22
Difficulty Level : Average

Ingredients:

- 3/4 cup of all-purpose flour
- 3/4 cup of whole wheat flour
- 2 tablespoons sugar
- 1 tablespoon of baking powder
- 1/8 teaspoon salt
- 1 teaspoon of pumpkin pie spice
- 2 cups of 100% bran cereal
- 1 1/2 cups of skim milk
- 2 egg whites
- 15 ounces x 1 can pumpkin
- 2 tablespoons of avocado oil

Directions:

Preheat the oven to 400 degrees Fahrenheit. Prepare a muffin pan enough for 22 muffins and line with a non-stick cooking spray. Stir together the first four ingredients until combined. Set aside.

Using a large mixing bowl, mix together milk and cereal bran and let it stand for 2 minutes or until the cereal softens. Add in the oil, egg whites, and pumpkin in the bran mix and blend well. Fill in the flour mixture and mix well.

Divide the batter into equal portions into the muffin pan. Bake for 20 minutes. Pull out the muffins from pan and serve warm or cooled.

Nutrition (for 100g): 70 Calories 3g Fat 14g Carbohydrates 3g Protein 484mg Sodium

Buckwheat Buttermilk Pancakes

Preparation Time : 2 minutes

Cooking Time : 18 minutes

Servings : 9

Difficulty Level : Easy

Ingredients:

- 1/2 cup of buckwheat flour
- 1/2 cup of all-purpose flour
- 2 teaspoons of baking powder
- 1 teaspoon of brown sugar
- 2 tablespoons of olive oil
- 2 large eggs
- 1 cup of reduced-fat buttermilk

Directions:

Incorporate the first four ingredients in a bowl. Add the oil, buttermilk, and eggs and mix until thoroughly blended. Put griddle over medium heat and spray with non-stick cooking spray. Pour ¼ cup of the batter over the skillet and cook for 1-2 minutes each side or until they turn golden brown. Serve immediately.

Nutrition (for 100g): 108 Calories 3g Fat 12g Carbohydrates 4g Protein 556mg Sodium

French Toast with Almonds and Peach Compote

Preparation Time : 10 minutes
Cooking Time : 15 minutes
Servings : 4
Difficulty Level : Easy

Ingredients:

- Compote:
- 3 tablespoons of sugar substitute, sucralose-based
- 1/3 cup + 2 tablespoons of water, divided
- 1 1/2 cups of fresh peeled or frozen, thawed and drained sliced peaches
- 2 tablespoons peach fruit spread, no-sugar-added
- 1/4 teaspoon of ground cinnamon
- Almond French toast
- 1/4 cup of (skim) fat-free milk
- 3 tablespoons of sugar substitute, sucralose-based
- 2 whole eggs
- 2 egg whites
- 1/2 teaspoon of almond extract
- 1/8 teaspoon salt
- 4 slices of multigrain bread
- 1/3 cup of sliced almonds

Directions:

To make the compote, dissolve 3 tablespoons sucralose in 1/3 cup of water in a medium saucepan over high-medium heat. Stir in the peaches and bring to a boil. Reduce the heat to medium and continue to cook uncovered for another 5 minutes or until the peaches softened.

Combine remaining water and fruit spread then stir into the peaches in the saucepan. Cook for another minute or until syrup thickens. Pull out from heat and add in the cinnamon. Cover to keep warm.

To make the French toast. Combine the milk and sucralose in a large size shallow dish and whisk until it completely dissolves. Whisk in the egg whites, eggs, almond extract and salt. Dip both sides of the bread slices for 3 minutes in the egg mixture or until completely soaked. Sprinkle both sides with sliced almonds and press firmly to adhere.

Brush the non-stick skillet with cooking spray and place over medium-high heat. Cook bread slices on griddle for 2 to 3 minutes both sides or until it turns light brown. Serve topped with the peach compote.

Nutrition (for 100g): 277 Calories 7g Fat 31g Carbohydrates 12g Protein 665mg Sodium

Mixed Berries Oatmeal with Sweet Vanilla Cream

Preparation Time : 5 minutes
Cooking Time : 5 minutes
Servings : 4
Difficulty Level : Easy

Ingredients:

- 2 cups water
- 1 cup of quick-cooking oats
- 1 tablespoon of sucralose-based sugar substitute
- 1/2 teaspoon of ground cinnamon
- 1/8 teaspoon salt
- <u>Cream</u>
- 3/4 cup of fat-free half-and-half
- 3 tablespoons of sucralose-based sugar substitute
- 1/2 teaspoon of vanilla extract
- 1/2 teaspoon of almond extract
- <u>Toppings</u>
- 1 1/2 cups of fresh blueberries
- 1/2 cup of fresh or frozen and thawed raspberries

Directions:

Boil water in high-heat and stir in the oats. Reduce heat to medium while cooking oats, uncovered for 2 minutes or until thick. Remove from heat and stir in sugar substitute, salt and cinnamon. In a medium size bowl, incorporate all the cream ingredients until well blended. Scoop cooked oatmeal into 4 equal portions and pour the sweet cream over. Top with the berries and serve.

Nutrition (for 100g): 150 Calories 5g Fat 30g Carbohydrates 5g Protein 807mg Sodium

Choco-Strawberry Crepe

Preparation Time : 5 minutes
Cooking Time : 10 minutes
Servings : 4
Difficulty Level : Easy

Ingredients:

- 1 cup of wheat all-purpose flour
- 2/3 cup of low-fat (1%) milk
- 2 egg whites
- 1 egg
- 3 tablespoons sugar
- 3 tablespoons of unsweetened cocoa powder
- 1 tablespoon of cooled melted butter
- 1/2 teaspoon salt
- 2 teaspoons of canola oil
- 3 tablespoons of strawberry fruit spread
- 3 1/2 cups of sliced thawed frozen or fresh strawberries
- 1/2 cup of fat-free thawed frozen whipped topping
- Fresh mint leaves (if desired)

Directions:

Incorporate the first eight ingredients in a large size bowl until smooth and thoroughly blended.

Brush ¼-teaspoon oil on a small size non-stick skillet over medium heat. Pour ¼-cup of the batter onto the center and swirl to coat the pan with batter.

Cook for a minute or until crêpe turns dull and the edges dry. Flip on the other side and cook for another half a minute. Repeat process with remaining mixture and oil.

Scoop ¼-cup of thawed strawberries at the center of the crepe and toll up to cover filling. Top with 2 tablespoons whipped cream and garnish with mint before serving.

Nutrition (for 100g): 334 Calories 5g Fat 58g Carbohydrates 10g Protein 678mg Sodium

No Crust Asparagus-Ham Quiche

Preparation Time : 5 minutes
Cooking Time : 42 minutes
Servings : 6
Difficulty Level : Easy

Ingredients:

- 2 cups 1/2-inched sliced asparagus
- 1 red chopped bell pepper
- 1 cup milk, low-fat (1%)
- 2 tablespoons of wheat all-purpose flour
- 4 egg whites
- 1 egg, whole
- 1 cup cooked chopped deli ham
- 2 tablespoons fresh chopped tarragon or basil
- 1/2 teaspoon of salt (optional)
- 1/4 teaspoon of black pepper
- 1/2 cup Swiss cheese, finely shredded

Directions:

Preheat your oven to 350 degrees F. Microwave bell pepper and asparagus in a tablespoon of water on HIGH for 2 minutes. Drain. Whisk flour and milk, and then add egg and egg whites until well combined. Stir in the vegetables and the remaining ingredients except the cheese.

Pour in a 9-inch size pie dish and bake for 35 minutes. Sprinkle cheese over the quiche and bake another 5 minutes or until cheese melts. Allow it cool for 5 minutes then cut into 6 wedges to serve.

Nutrition (for 100g): 138 Calories 1g Fat 8g Carbohydrates 13g Protein 588mg Sodium

Apple Cheese Scones

Preparation Time : 20 minutes
Cooking Time : 15 minutes
Servings : 10
Difficulty Level : Average

Ingredients:

- 1 cup of all-purpose flour
- 1 cup whole wheat flour, white
- 3 tablespoons sugar
- 1 1/2 teaspoons of baking powder
- 1/2 teaspoon salt
- 1/2 teaspoon of ground cinnamon
- 1/4 teaspoon of baking soda
- 1 diced Granny Smith apple
- 1/2 cup shredded sharp Cheddar cheese
- 1/3 cup applesauce, natural or unsweetened
- 1/4 cup milk, fat-free (skim)
- 3 tablespoons of melted butter
- 1 egg

Directions:

Prepare your oven to 425 degrees F. Ready the baking sheet by lining with parchment paper. Merge all dry ingredients in a bowl and mix. Stir in the cheese and apple. Set aside. Whisk all the wet ingredients together. Pour over the dry mixture until blended and turns like a sticky dough.

Work on the dough on a floured surface about 5 times. Pat and then stretch into an 8-inch circle. Slice into 10 diagonal cuts.

Place on the baking sheet and spray top with cooking spray. Bake for 15 minutes or until lightly golden. Serve.

Nutrition (for 100g): 169 Calories 2g Fat 26g Carbohydrates 5g Protein 689mg Sodium

Bacon and Egg Wrap

Preparation Time : 15 minutes
Cooking Time : 15 minutes
Servings : 4
Difficulty Level : Easy

Ingredients:

- 1 cup egg substitute, cholesterol-free
- 1/4 cup Parmesan cheese, shredded
- 2 slices diced Canadian bacon
- 1/2 teaspoon red hot pepper sauce
- 1/4 teaspoon of black pepper
- 4x7-inch whole wheat tortillas
- 1 cup of baby spinach leaves

Directions:

Preheat your oven at 325 degrees F. Combine the first five ingredients to make the filling. Pour the mixture in a 9-inch glass dish sprayed with butter-flavored cooking spray.

Bake for 15 minutes or until egg sets. Remove from oven. Place the tortillas for a minute in the oven. Cut baked egg mixture into quarters. Arrange one quarter at the center of each tortillas and top with ¼-cup spinach. Fold tortilla from the bottom to the center and then both sides to the center to enclose. Serve immediately.

Nutrition (for 100g): 195 Calories 3g Fat 20g Carbohydrates 15g Protein 688mg Sodium

Orange-Blueberry Muffin

Preparation Time : 10 minutes

Cooking Time : 10-25 minutes

Servings : 12

Difficulty Level : Average

Ingredients:

- 1 3/4 cups of all-purpose flour
- 1/3 cup sugar
- 2 1/2 teaspoons of baking powder
- 1/2 teaspoon of baking soda
- 1/2 teaspoon salt
- 1/2 teaspoon of ground cinnamon
- 3/4 cup milk, fat-free (skim)
- 1/4 cup butter
- 1 egg, large, lightly beaten
- 3 tablespoons thawed orange juice concentrate
- 1 teaspoon vanilla
- 3/4 cup fresh blueberries

Directions:

Ready your oven to 400 degrees F. Follow steps 2 to 5 of Buckwheat Apple-Raisin Muffin Fill up the muffin cups ¾-full of the mixture and bake for 20 to 25 minutes. Let it cool 5 minutes and serve warm.

Nutrition (for 100g): 149 Calories 5g Fat 24g Carbohydrates 3g Protein 518mg Sodium

14. Baked Ginger Oatmeal with Pear Topping

Preparation Time : 10 minutes
Cooking Time : 15 minutes
Servings : 2
Difficulty Level : Easy

Ingredients:

- 1 cup of old-fashioned oats
- 3/4 cup milk, fat-free (skim)
- 1 egg white
- 1 1/2 teaspoons grated ginger, fresh or 3/4 teaspoon of ground ginger
- 2 tablespoons brown sugar, divided
- 1/2 ripe diced pear

Directions:

Spray 2x6 ounce ramekins with a non-stick cooking spray. Prepare the oven to 350 degrees F. Combine the first four ingredients and a tablespoon of sugar then mix well. Pour evenly between the 2 ramekins. Top with pear slices and the remaining tablespoon of sugar. Bake for 15 minutes. Serve warm.

Nutrition (for 100g): 268 Calories 5g fat 2g Carbohydrates 10g Protein 779mg Sodium

Greek Style Veggie Omelet

Preparation Time : 10 minutes

Cooking Time : 20 minutes

Servings : 2

Difficulty Level : Easy

Ingredients:

- 4 large eggs
- 2 tablespoons of fat-free milk
- 1/8 teaspoon salt
- 3 teaspoons of olive oil, divided
- 2 cups baby Portobello, sliced
- 1/4 cup of finely chopped onion
- 1 cup of fresh baby spinach
- 3 tablespoons feta cheese, crumbled
- 2 tablespoons ripe olives, sliced
- Freshly ground pepper

Directions:

Whisk together first three ingredients. Stir in 2 tablespoons of oil in a non-stick skillet over medium-high heat. Sauté the onions and mushroom for 5-6 minutes or until golden brown. Mix in the spinach and cook. Remove mixture from pan.

Using the same pan, heat over medium-low heat the remaining oil. Pour your egg mixture and as it starts to set, pushed the edges towards the center to let the uncooked mixture flow underneath. When eggs set scoop the veggie mixture on one side. Sprinkle with olives and feta then fold the other side to close. Slice in half and sprinkle with pepper to serve.

Nutrition (for 100g): 271 Calories 2g Fat 7g Carbohydrates 18g Protein 648mg Sodium

Summer Smoothie

Preparation Time : 8 minutes

Cooking Time : 0 minutes

Servings : 2

Difficulty Level : Easy

Ingredients:

- 1/2 Banana, Peeled
- 2 Cups Strawberries, Halved
- 3 Tablespoons Mint, Chopped
- 1 1/2 Cups Coconut Water
- 1/2 Avocado, Pitted & Peeled
- 1 Date, Chopped
- Ice Cubes as Needed

Directions:

Incorporate everything in a blender, and process until smooth. Add ice cubes to thicken, and serve chilled.

Nutrition (for 100g): 360 calories 12g fats 5g carbohydrates 31g protein 737mg sodium

Ham & Egg Pitas

Preparation Time : 5 minutes

Cooking Time : 15 minutes

Servings : 4

Difficulty Level : Easy

Ingredients:

- 6 Eggs
- 2 Shallots, Chopped
- 1 Teaspoon Olive Oil
- 1/3 Cup Smoked Ham, Chopped
- 1/3 Cup Sweet Green Pepper, Chopped
- 1/4 Cup Brie Cheese
- Sea Salt & Black Pepper to Taste
- 4 Lettuce Leaves
- 2 Pita Breads, Whole Wheat

Directions:

Heat the olive oil in a pan using medium heat. Add in your shallots and green pepper, letting them cook for five minutes while stirring frequently.

Get out a bowl and whip your eggs, sprinkling in your salt and pepper. Make sure your eggs are well beaten. Put the eggs into the pan, and then mix in the ham and cheese. Stir well, and cook until your mixture thickens. Split the pitas in half, and open the pockets.

Spread a teaspoon of mustard in each pocket, and add a lettuce leaf in each one. Spread the egg mixture in each one and serve.

Nutrition (for 100g): 610 calories 21g fats 10g carbohydrates 41g protein 807mg sodium

Breakfast Couscous

Preparation Time : 5 minutes

Cooking Time : 15 minutes

Servings : 4

Difficulty Level : Average

Ingredients:

- 3 Cups Milk, Low Fat
- 1 Cinnamon Stick
- 1/2 Cup Apricots, Dried & Chopped
- 1/4 Cup Currants, Dried
- 1 Cup Couscous, Uncooked
- Pinch Sea Salt, Fine
- 4 Teaspoons Butter, Melted
- 6 Teaspoons Brown Sugar

Directions:

Heat a pan up with milk and cinnamon using medium-high heat. Cook for three minutes before removing the pan from heat.

Add in your apricots, couscous, salt, currants, and sugar. Stir well, and then cover. Leave it to the side, and let it sit for fifteen minutes.

Throw out the cinnamon stick, and divide between bowls. Sprinkle with brown sugar before serving.

Nutrition (for 100g): 520 calories 28g fats 10g carbohydrates 39g protein 619mg sodium

Peach Breakfast Salad

Preparation Time : 10 minutes

Cooking Time : 0 minutes

Servings : 1

Difficulty Level : Easy

Ingredients:

- 1/4 Cup Walnuts, Chopped & Toasted
- 1 Teaspoon Honey, Raw
- 1 Peach, Pitted & Sliced
- 1/2 Cup Cottage Cheese, Nonfat & Room Temperature
- 1 Tablespoon Mint, Fresh & Chopped
- 1 Lemon, Zested

Directions:

Place your cottage cheese in a bowl, and top with peach slices and walnuts. Drizzle with honey, and top with mint.

Sprinkle on your lemon zest before serving immediately.

Nutrition (for 100g): 280 calories 11g fats 19g carbohydrates 39g protein 527mg sodium

Savory Oats

Preparation Time : 10 minutes
Cooking Time : 10 minutes
Servings : 2
Difficulty Level : Easy

Ingredients:

- 1/2 Cup Steel Cut Oats
- 1 Cup Water
- 1 Tomato, Large & Chopped
- 1 Cucumber, Chopped
- 1 Tablespoon Olive Oil
- Sea Salt & Black Pepper to Taste
- Flat Leaf Parsley, Chopped to Garnish
- Parmesan Cheese, Low Fat & Freshly Grated

Directions:

Bring your oats and a cup of water to a boil using a saucepan over high heat. Stir often until your water is completely absorbed, which will take roughly fifteen minutes. Divide between two bowls, and top with tomatoes and cucumber. Drizzle with olive oil and top with parmesan. Garnish with parsley before serving.

Nutrition (for 100g): 408 calories 13g fats 10g carbohydrates 28g protein 825mg sodium

Tahini & Apple Toast

Preparation Time : 15 minutes
Cooking Time : 0 minutes
Servings : 1
Difficulty Level : Easy

Ingredients:

- 2 Tablespoons Tahini
- 2 Slices Whole Wheat Bread, Toasted
- 1 Teaspoon Honey, Raw
- 1 Apple, Small, Cored & Sliced Thin

Directions:

Start by spreading the tahini over your toast, and then lay your apples over it. drizzle with honey before serving.

Nutrition (for 100g): 366 calories 13g fats 9g carbohydrates 29g protein 686mg sodium

Scrambled Basil Eggs

Preparation Time : 5 minutes
Cooking Time : 10 minutes
Servings : 2
Difficulty Level : Easy

Ingredients:

- 4 Eggs, Large
- 2 Tablespoons Fresh Basil, Chopped Fine
- 2 Tablespoons Gruyere Cheese, Grated
- 1 Tablespoon Cream
- 1 Tablespoon Olive Oil
- 2 Cloves Garlic, Minced
- Sea Salt & Black Pepper to Taste

Directions:

Get out a large bowl and beat your basil, cheese, cream and eggs together. Whisk until it's well combined. Get out a large skillet over medium-low heat, and heat your oil. Add in your garlic, cooking for a minute. It should turn golden.

Pour the egg mixture into your skillet over the garlic, and then continue to scramble as they cook so they become soft and fluffy. Season it well and serve warm.

Nutrition (for 100g): 360 calories 14g fats 8g carbohydrates 29g protein 545mg sodium

Greek Potatoes & Eggs

Preparation Time : 10 minutes

Cooking Time : 30 minutes

Servings : 2

Difficulty Level : Easy

Ingredients:

- 3 tomatoes, seeded & roughly chopped
- 2 tablespoons basil, fresh & chopped
- 1 clove garlic, minced
- 2 tablespoons + ½ cup olive oil, divided
- sea salt & black pepper to taste
- 3 russet potatoes, large
- 4 eggs, large
- 1 teaspoon oregano, fresh & chopped

Directions:

Get the food processor and place your tomatoes in, pureeing them with the skin on.

Add your garlic, two tablespoons of oil, salt, pepper and basil. Pulse until it's well combined. Place this mixture in a skillet, cooking while covered for twenty to twenty-five minutes over low heat. Your sauce should be thickened as well as bubbly.

Dice your potatoes into cubes, and then place them in a skillet with a ½ a cup of olive oil in a skillet using medium-low heat.

Fry your potatoes until crisp and browned. This should take five minutes, and then cover the skillet, reducing the heat to low. Steam them until your potatoes are done.

Stir in the eggs into the tomato sauce, and cook using low heat for six minutes. Your eggs should be set.

Remove the potatoes from your pan, and drain using paper towels. Place them in a bowl. Sprinkle in your salt, pepper and oregano, and then serve your eggs with potatoes. Drizzle your sauce over the mixture, and serve warm.

Nutrition (for 100g): 348 calories 12g fats 7g carbohydrates 27g protein 469mg sodium

Avocado & Honey Smoothie

Preparation Time : 5 minutes

Cooking Time : 0 minutes

Servings : 2

Difficulty Level : Easy

Ingredients:

- 1 1/2 cups soy milk
- 1 avocado, large
- 2 tablespoons honey, raw

Directions:

Incorporate all ingredients together and blend until smooth, and serve immediately.

Nutrition (for 100g): 280 calories 19g fats 11g carbohydrates 30g protein 547mg sodium

Vegetable Frittata

Preparation Time : 5 minutes
Cooking Time : 10 minutes
Servings : 2
Difficulty Level : Easy

Ingredients:

- 1/2 baby eggplant, peeled & diced
- 1 handful baby spinach leaves
- 1 tablespoon olive oil
- 3 eggs, large
- 1 teaspoon almond milk
- 1-ounce goat cheese, crumbled
- 1/4 small red pepper, chopped
- sea salt & black pepper to taste

Directions:

Start by heating the broiler on your oven, and then beat the eggs together with almond milk. Make sure it's well combined, and then get out a nonstick, oven proof skillet. Place it over medium-high heat, and then add in your olive oil.

Once your oil is heated, add in your eggs. Spread your spinach over this mixture in an even layer, and top with the rest of your vegetables.

Reduce your heat to medium, and sprinkle with salt and pepper. Allow your vegetables and eggs to cook for five minutes. The bottom half of your eggs should be firm, and your vegetables should be tender. Top with goat cheese, and then broil on the middle rack for three to five minutes. Your eggs should be all the way done, and your cheese should be melted. Slice into wedges and serve warm.

Nutrition (for 100g): 340 calories 16g fats 9g carbohydrates 37g protein 748mg sodium

Mini Lettuce Wraps

Preparation Time : 15 minutes
Cooking Time : 0 minutes
Servings : 4
Difficulty Level : Easy

Ingredients:

- 1 cucumber, diced
- 1 red onion, sliced
- 1-ounce feta cheese, low fat & crumbed
- 1 lemon, juiced
- 1 tomato, diced
- 1 tablespoon olive oil
- 12 small iceberg lettuce leaves
- sea salt & black pepper to taste

Directions:

Combine your tomato, onion, feta, and cucumber in a bowl. Mix your oil and juice, and season with salt and pepper.

Fill each leaf with the vegetable mixture, and roll them tightly. Use a toothpick to keep them together to serve.

Nutrition (for 100g): 291 calories 10g fats 9g carbohydrates 27g protein 655mg sodium

Curry Apple Couscous

Preparation Time : 20 minutes

Cooking Time : 5 minutes

Servings : 4

Difficulty Level : Average

Ingredients:

- 2 teaspoons olive oil
- 2 leeks, white parts only, sliced
- 1 apple, diced
- 2 tablespoons curry powder
- 2 cups couscous, cooked & whole wheat
- 1/2 cup pecans, chopped

Directions:

Heat your oil in a skillet using medium heat. Add the leeks, and cook until tender, which will take five minutes. Add in your apple, and cook until soft.

Add in your curry powder and couscous, and stir well. Remove from heat, and mix in your nuts before serving immediately.

Nutrition (for 100g): 330 calories 12g fats 8g carbohydrates 30g protein 824mg sodium

Lamb & Vegetable Bake

Preparation Time : 20 minutes

Cooking Time : 1 hour and 10 minutes

Servings : 8

Difficulty Level : Average

Ingredients:

- 1/4 cup olive oil
- 1 lb. lean lamb, boneless & chopped into ½ inch pieces
- 2 red potatoes, large, scrubbed & diced
- 1 onion, chopped roughly
- 2 cloves garlic, minced
- 28 ounces diced tomatoes with liquid, canned & no salt
- 2 zucchinis, cut into ½ inch slices
- 1 red bell pepper, seeded & cut into 1-inch cubes
- 2 tablespoons flat leaf parsley, chopped
- 1 tablespoon paprika
- 1 teaspoon thyme
- 1/2 teaspoon cinnamon
- 1/2 cup red wine
- sea salt & black pepper to taste

Directions:

Start by turning the oven to 325, and then get out a large stew pot. Place it over medium-high heat to heat your olive oil. Once your oil is hot stir in your lamb, browning the meat. Stir frequently to keep it from running, and then place your lamb in a baking dish. Cook your garlic, onion and potatoes in the skillet until they're tender, which should take five to six minutes more. Place them to the baking dish as well. Pour the zucchini, pepper, and tomatoes in the pan with your herbs and spices. Allow it to simmer for ten minutes more before pouring it into your baking dish. Pour in the wine and pepper sauce. Add in your tomato, and then cover with foil. Bake for an hour. Take the cover off for the last fifteen minutes of baking, and adjust seasoning as needed.

Nutrition (for 100g): 240 calories 14g fats 8g carbohydrates 36g protein 427mg sodium

Herb Flounder

Preparation Time : 20 minutes
Cooking Time : 1 hour and 5 minutes
Servings : 4
Difficulty Level : Average

Ingredients:

- 1/2 cup flatleaf parsley, lightly packed
- 1/4 cup olive oil
- 4 cloves garlic, peeled & halved
- 2 tablespoons rosemary, fresh
- 2 tablespoons thyme leaves, fresh
- 2 tablespoons sage, fresh
- 2 tablespoons lemon zest, fresh
- 4 flounder fillets
- sea salt & black pepper to taste

Directions:

Ready your oven to 350, and then put all of the ingredients except for the flounder in the processor. Blend until it forms at hick paste. Put your fillets on a baking sheet, and brush them down with the paste. Allow them to chill in the fridge for an hour. Bake for ten minutes. Season and serve warm.

Nutrition (for 100g): 307 calories 11g fats 7g carbohydrates 34g protein 824mg sodium

Cauliflower Quinoa

Preparation Time : 15 minutes
Cooking Time : 10 minutes
Servings : 4
Difficulty Level : Easy

Ingredients:

- 1 1/2 cups quinoa, cooked
- 3 tablespoons olive oil
- 3 cups cauliflower florets
- 2 spring onions, chopped
- 1 tablespoon red wine vinegar
- sea salt & black pepper to taste
- 1 tablespoon red wine vinegar
- 1 tablespoon chives, chopped
- 1 tablespoon parsley, chopped

Directions:

Start by heating up a pan over medium-high heat. Add your oil. Once your oil is hot, add in your spring onions and cook for about two minutes. Add in your quinoa and cauliflower, and then add in the rest of the ingredients. Mix well, and cover. Cook for nine minutes over medium heat, and divide between plates to serve.

Nutrition (for 100g): 290 calories 14g fats 9g carbohydrates 26g protein 656mg sodium

Mango Pear Smoothie

Preparation Time : 5 minutes

Cooking Time : 0 minutes

Servings : 1

Difficulty Level : Easy

Ingredients:

- 2 ice cubes
- ½ cup Greek yogurt, plain
- ½ mango, peeled, pitted & chopped
- 1 cup kale, chopped
- 1 pear, ripe, cored & chopped

Directions:

Blend together until thick and smooth. Serve chilled.

Nutrition (for 100g): 350 calories 12g fats 9g carbohydrates 40g protein 457mg sodium

Spinach Omelet

Preparation Time : 10 minutes

Cooking Time : 20 minutes

Servings : 4

Difficulty Level : Easy

Ingredients:

- 3 tablespoons olive oil
- 1 onion, small & chopped
- 1 clove garlic, minced
- 4 tomatoes, large, cored & chopped
- 1 teaspoon sea salt, fine
- 8 eggs, beaten
- ¼ teaspoon black pepper
- 2 ounces feta cheese, crumbled
- 1 tablespoon flat leaf parsley, fresh & chopped

Directions:

Preheat oven to 400 degrees, and pour olive oil in an ovenproof skillet. Place your skillet over high heat, adding in your onions. Cook for five to seven minutes. Your onions should soften.

Add your tomatoes, salt, pepper and garlic in. Then simmer for another five minutes, and fill in your beaten eggs. Mix lightly, and cook for three to five minutes. They should set at the bottom. Put the pan in the oven, baking for five minutes more. Remove from the oven, topping with parsley and feta. Serve warm.

Nutrition (for 100g): 280 calories 19g fats 10g carbohydrates 31g protein 625mg sodium

Almond Pancakes

Preparation Time : 15 minutes

Cooking Time : 15 minutes

Servings : 6

Difficulty Level : Easy

Ingredients:

- 2 cups almond milk, unsweetened & room temperature
- 2 eggs, large & room temperature
- ½ cup coconut oil, melted + more for greasing
- 2 teaspoons honey, raw
- ¼ teaspoon sea salt, fine
- ½ teaspoon baking soda
- 1 ½ cups whole wheat flour
- ½ cup almond flour
- 1 ½ teaspoons baking powder
- ¼ teaspoon cinnamon, ground

Directions:

Get out a large bowl and whisk your coconut oil, eggs, almond milk and honey, blending until it's mixed well.

Get a medium bowl out and sift together your baking powder, baking soda, almond flour, sea salt, whole wheat flour and cinnamon. Mix well.

Add your flour mixture to your milk mixture, and whisk well.

Get out a large skillet and grease it using your coconut oil before placing it over medium-high heat. Add in your pancake batter in ½ cup measurements.

Cook for three minutes or until the edges are firm. The bottom of your pancake should be golden, and bubbles should break the surface. Cook both sides.

Wipe clean your skillet, and repeat until all of your batter is used. Make sure to re-grease your skillet, and top with fresh fruit if desired.

Nutrition (for 100g): 205 calories 16g fats 9g carbohydrates 36g protein 828mg sodium

Quinoa Fruit Salad

Preparation Time : 25 minutes
Cooking Time : 0 minutes
Servings : 4
Difficulty Level : Easy

Ingredients:

- 2 tablespoons honey, raw
- 1 cup strawberries, fresh & sliced
- 2 tablespoons lime juice, fresh
- 1 teaspoon basil, fresh & chopped
- 1 cup quinoa, cooked
- 1 mango, peeled, pitted & diced
- 1 cup blackberries, fresh
- 1 peach, pitted & diced
- 2 kiwis, peeled & quartered

Directions:

Start by mixing your lime juice, basil and honey together in a small bowl. In a different bowl mix your strawberries, quinoa, blackberries, peach, kiwis and mango. Add in your honey mixture, and toss to coat before serving.

Nutrition (for 100g): 159 calories 12g fats 9g carbohydrates 29g protein 829mg sodium

Strawberry Rhubarb Smoothie

Preparation Time : 8 minutes
Cooking Time : 0 minutes
Servings : 1
Difficulty Level : Easy

Ingredients:

- 1 cup strawberries, fresh & sliced
- 1 rhubarb stalk, chopped
- 2 tablespoons honey, raw
- 3 ice cubes
- 1/8 teaspoon ground cinnamon
- ½ cup Greek yogurt, plain

Directions:

Start by getting out a small saucepan and fill it with water. Place it over high heat to bring it to a boil, and then add in your rhubarb. Boil for three minutes before draining and transferring it to a blender.

In your blender add in your yogurt, honey, cinnamon and strawberries. Once smooth, stir in your ice. Blend until there are no lumps and it's thick. Enjoy cold.

Nutrition (for 100g): 201 calories 11g fats 9g carbohydrates 39g protein 657mg sodium

Barley Porridge

Preparation Time : 10 minutes

Cooking Time : 20 minutes

Servings : 4

Difficulty Level : Easy

Ingredients:

- 1 cup wheat berries
- 1 cup barley
- 2 cups almond milk, unsweetened + more for serving
- ½ cup blueberries
- ½ cup pomegranate seeds
- 2 cups water
- ½ cup hazelnuts, toasted & chopped
- ¼ cup honey, raw

Directions:

Get out a saucepan, put it over medium-high heat, and then add in your almond milk, water, barley and wheat berries. Let it boil before lowering the heat and allow it to simmer for twenty-five minutes. Stir frequently. Your grains should become tender.

Top each serving with blueberries, pomegranate seeds, hazelnuts, a tablespoon of honey and a splash of almond milk.

Nutrition (for 100g): 150 calories 10g fats 9g carbohydrates 29g protein 546mg sodium

Gingerbread & Pumpkin Smoothie

Preparation Time : 15 minutes

Cooking Time : 50 minutes

Servings : 1

Difficulty Level : Easy

Ingredients:

- 1 cup almond milk, unsweetened
- 2 teaspoons chia seeds
- 1 banana
- ½ cup pumpkin puree, canned
- ¼ teaspoon ginger, ground
- ¼ teaspoon cinnamon, ground
- 1/8 teaspoon nutmeg, ground

Directions:

Start by getting out a bowl and mix your chai seeds and almond milk. Allow them to soak for at least an hour, but you can soak them overnight. Transfer them to a blender.

Add in your remaining ingredients, and then blend until smooth. Serve chilled.

Nutrition (for 100g): 250 calories 13g fats 7g carbohydrates 26g protein 621mg sodium

Green Juice

Preparation Time : 5 minutes

Cooking Time : 0 minutes

Servings : 1

Difficulty Level : Easy

Ingredients:

- 3 cups dark leafy greens
- 1 cucumber
- ¼ cup fresh Italian parsley leaves
- ¼ pineapple, cut into wedges
- ½ green apple
- ½ orange
- ½ lemon
- Pinch grated fresh ginger

Directions:

Using a juicer, run the greens, cucumber, parsley, pineapple, apple, orange, lemon, and ginger through it, pour into a large cup, and serve.

Nutrition (for 100g): 200 calories 14g fats 6g carbohydrates 27g protein 541mg sodium

Walnut & Date Smoothie

Preparation Time : 10 minutes

Cooking Time : 0 minutes

Servings : 2

Difficulty Level : Easy

Ingredients:

- 4 dates, pitted
- ½ cup milk
- 2 cups Greek yogurt, plain
- 1/2 cup walnuts
- ½ teaspoon cinnamon, ground
- ½ teaspoon vanilla extract, pure
- 2-3 ice cubes

Directions:

Blend everything together until smooth, and then serve chilled.

Nutrition (for 100g): 109 calories 11g fats 7g carbohydrates 29g protein 732mg sodium

Fruit Smoothie

Preparation Time : 5 minutes
Cooking Time : 0 minutes
Servings : 2
Difficulty Level : Easy

Ingredients:

- 2 cups blueberries
- 2 cups unsweetened almond milk
- 1 cup crushed ice
- ½ teaspoon ground ginger

Directions:

Put the blueberries, almond milk, ice, and ginger in a blender. Process until smooth.

Nutrition (for 100g): 115 calories 10g fats 5g carbohydrates 27g protein 912mg sodium

Chocolate Banana Smoothie

Preparation Time : 5 minutes

Cooking Time : 0 minutes

Servings : 2

Difficulty Level : Easy

Ingredients:

- 2 bananas, peeled
- 1 cup skim milk
- 1 cup crushed ice
- 3 tablespoons unsweetened cocoa powder
- 3 tablespoons honey

Directions:

In a blender, mix the bananas, almond milk, ice, cocoa powder, and honey. Blend until smooth.

Nutrition (for 100g): 150 calories 18g fats 6g carbohydrates 30g protein 821mg sodium

Yogurt with Blueberries, Honey, and Mint

Preparation Time : 5 minutes

Cooking Time : 0 minutes

Servings : 2

Difficulty Level : Easy

Ingredients:

- 2 cups unsweetened nonfat plain Greek yogurt
- 1 cup blueberries
- 3 tablespoons honey
- 2 tablespoons fresh mint leaves, chopped

Directions:

Apportion the yogurt between 2 small bowls. Top with the blueberries, honey, and mint.

Nutrition (for 100g): 126 calories 12g fats 8g carbohydrates 37g protein 932mg sodium

Berry and Yogurt Parfait

Preparation Time : 5 minutes

Cooking Time : 0 minutes

Servings : 2

Difficulty Level : Easy

Ingredients:

- 1 cup raspberries
- 1½ cups unsweetened nonfat plain Greek yogurt
- 1 cup blackberries
- ¼ cup chopped walnuts

Directions:

In 2 bowls, layer the raspberries, yogurt, and blackberries. Sprinkle with the walnuts.

Nutrition (for 100g): 119 calories 13g fats 7g carbohydrates 28g protein 732mg sodium

Oatmeal with Berries and Sunflower Seeds

Preparation Time : 5 minutes

Cooking Time : 10 minutes

Servings : 4

Difficulty Level : Easy

Ingredients:

- 1¾ cups water
- ½ cup unsweetened almond milk
- Pinch sea salt
- 1 cup old-fashioned oats
- ½ cup blueberries
- ½ cup raspberries
- ¼ cup sunflower seeds

Directions:

Boil water with almond milk, and sea salt in a medium saucepan over medium-high heat.

Stir in the oats. Decrease the heat to medium-low and continue stirring and cook, for 5 minutes. Cover, and let the oatmeal stand for 2 minutes more. Stir and serve topped with the blueberries, raspberries, and sunflower seeds.

Nutrition (for 100g): 106 calories 9g fats 8g carbohydrates 29g protein 823mg sodium

Almond and Maple Quick Grits

Preparation Time : 5 minutes

Cooking Time : 10 minutes

Servings : 4

Difficulty Level : Easy

Ingredients:

- 1½ cups water
- ½ cup unsweetened almond milk
- Pinch sea salt
- ½ cup quick-cooking grits
- ½ teaspoon ground cinnamon
- ¼ cup pure maple syrup
- ¼ cup slivered almonds

Directions:

Put water, almond milk, and sea salt in a medium saucepan over medium-high heat and wait to boil.

Stir continuously with a wooden spoon, slowly add the grits. Continue stirring to prevent lumps and bring the mixture to a slow boil. Reduce the heat to medium-low. Simmer for few minutes, stirring regularly, until the water is completely absorbed. Stir in the cinnamon, syrup, and almonds. Cook for 1 minute more, stirring.

Nutrition (for 100g): 126 calories 10g fats 7g carbohydrates 28g protein 851mg sodium

Banana Oats

Preparation Time : 10 minutes

Cooking Time : 10 minutes

Servings : 2

Difficulty Level : Easy

Ingredients:

- 1 banana, peeled and sliced
- ¾ c. almond milk
- ½ c. cold-brewed coffee
- 2 pitted dates
- 2 tbsps. cocoa powder
- 1 c. rolled oats
- 1 ½ tbsps. chia seeds

Directions:

Using a blender, add in all ingredients. Process well for 5 minutes and serve.

Nutrition (for 100g): 288 Calories 4.4g Fat 10g Carbohydrates 5.9g Protein 733mg Sodium

Breakfast Sandwich

Preparation Time : 5 minutes

Cooking Time : 20 minutes

Servings : 4

Difficulty Level : Easy

Ingredients:

- 4 multigrain sandwich thins
- 4 tsps. olive oil
- 4 eggs
- 1 tbsp. rosemary, fresh
- 2 c. baby spinach leaves, fresh
- 1 tomato, sliced
- 1 tbsp. of feta cheese
- Pinch of kosher salt
- Ground black pepper

Directions:

Prepare oven at 375 F/190 C. Brush the thins' sides with 2 tsps. of olive oil and set on a baking sheet. Set in the oven and toast for 5 minutes or until the edges are lightly brown.

In a skillet, add in the rest of the olive oil and rosemary to heat over high heat. Break and place whole eggs one at a time into the skillet. The yolk should still be runny, but the egg whites should be set.

Break yolks up with a spatula. Flip the egg and cook on another side until done. Remove eggs from heat. Place toasted sandwich thins on 4 separate plates. Divine spinach among the thins.

Top each thin with two tomato slices, cooked egg, and 1 tbsp. of feta cheese. Lightly sprinkle with salt and pepper for flavoring. Place remaining sandwich thin halves over the top and they are ready to serve.

Nutrition (for 100g): 241 Calories 12.2g Fat 60.2g Carbohydrates 21g Protein 855mg Sodium

Morning Couscous

Preparation Time : 10 minutes
Cooking Time : 8 minutes
Servings : 4
Difficulty Level : Average

Ingredients:

- 3 c. low-fat milk
- 1 c. whole-wheat couscous, uncooked
- 1 cinnamon stick
- ½ chopped apricot, dried
- ¼ c. currants, dried
- 6 tsps. brown sugar
- ¼ tsp. salt
- 4 tsps. melted butter

Directions:

Take a large saucepan and combine milk and cinnamon stick and heat over medium. Heat for 3 minutes or until microbubbles forms around edges of the pan. Do not boil. Remove from heat, stir in the couscous, apricots, currants, salt, and 4 tsps. brown sugar. Cover the mixture and allow it to sit for 15 minutes. Remove and throw away the cinnamon stick. Divide couscous among 4 bowls, and top each with 1 tsp. melted butter and ½ tsp. brown sugar. Ready to serve.

Nutrition (for 100g): 306 Calories 6g Fat 5g Carbohydrates 9g Protein 944mg Sodium

Avocado and Apple Smoothie

Preparation Time : 5 minutes

Cooking Time : 0 minutes

Servings : 2

Difficulty Level : Easy

Ingredients:

- 3 c. spinach
- 1 cored green apple, chopped
- 1 pitted avocado, peeled and chopped
- 3 tbsps. chia seeds
- 1 tsp. honey
- 1 frozen banana, peeled
- 2 c. coconut water

Directions:

Using your blender, add in all the ingredients. Process well for 5 minutes to obtain a smooth consistency and serve in glasses.

Nutrition (for 100g): 208 Calories 10.1g Fat 6g Carbohydrates 7g Protein 924mg Sodium

Mini Frittatas

Preparation Time : 10 minutes
Cooking Time : 20 minutes
Servings : 8
Difficulty Level : Easy

Ingredients:

- 1 chopped yellow onion
- 1 c. grated parmesan
- 1 chopped yellow bell pepper
- 1 chopped red bell pepper
- 1 chopped zucchini
- Salt and black pepper
- A drizzle of olive oil
- 8 whisked eggs
- 2 tbsps. chopped chives

Directions:

Set a pan over medium-high heat. Add in oil to warm. Stir in all ingredients except chives and eggs. Sauté for around 5 minutes.

Put the eggs on a muffin pan and top by the chives. Set oven to 350 F/176 C. Place the muffin pan into the oven to bake for about 10 minutes. Serve the eggs on a plate with sautéed vegetables.

Nutrition (for 100g): 55 Calories 3g Fat 0.7g Carbohydrates 9g Protein 844mg Sodium

Sun-dried Tomatoes Oatmeal

Preparation Time : 10 minutes
Cooking Time : 25 minutes
Servings : 4
Difficulty Level : Easy

Ingredients:

- 3 c. water
- 1 c. almond milk
- 1 tbsp. olive oil
- 1 c. steel-cut oats
- ¼ c. chopped tomatoes, sun-dried
- A pinch of red pepper flakes

Directions:

Using a pan, add water and milk to mix. Set on medium heat and allow to boil. Set up another pan on medium-high heat. Warm oil and add oats to cook for 2 minutes. Transfer to the first pan plus tomatoes then stir. Let simmer for approximately 20 minutes. Set in serving bowls and top with red pepper flakes. Enjoy.

Nutrition (for 100g): 170 Calories 17.8g Fat 1.5g Carbohydrates 10g Protein 645mg Sodium

Breakfast Egg on Avocado

Preparation Time : 5 minutes

Cooking Time : 15 minutes

Servings : 6

Difficulty Level : Easy

Ingredients:

- 1 tsp. garlic powder
- ½ tsp. sea salt
- ¼ c. shredded Parmesan cheese
- ¼ tsp. black pepper
- 3 pitted avocados, halved
- 6 eggs

Directions:

Ready the muffin tins and prepare the oven at 350 F/176 C. Split the avocado. To ensure that the egg would fit inside the avocado's cavity, lightly scrape off 1/3 of the meat.

Place avocado on a muffin tin to ensure that it faces with the top-up. Evenly season each avocado with pepper, salt, and garlic powder. Add one egg on each avocado cavity and garnish tops with cheese. Set in your oven to bake until the egg white is set, about 15 minutes. Serve and enjoy.

Nutrition (for 100g): 252 Calories 20g Fat 2g Carbohydrates 5g Protein 946mg Sodium

Brekky Egg- Potato Hash

Preparation Time : 10 minutes
Cooking Time : 25 minutes
Servings : 2
Difficulty Level : Easy

Ingredients:

- 1 zucchini, diced
- ½ c. chicken broth
- ½ lb. or 220 g cooked chicken
- 1 tbsp. olive oil
- 4 oz. or 113g shrimp
- Salt and black pepper
- 1 diced sweet potato
- 2 eggs
- ¼ tsp. cayenne pepper
- 2 tsps. garlic powder
- 1 c. fresh spinach

Directions:

In a skillet, add the olive oil. Fry the shrimp, cooked chicken and sweet potato for 2 minutes. Add the cayenne pepper, garlic powder and toss for 4 minutes. Add the zucchini and toss for another 3 minutes.

Whisk the eggs in a bowl and add to the skillet. Season using salt and pepper. Cover with the lid. Cook for 1 more minute and mix in the chicken broth.

Cover and cook for another 8 minutes on high heat. Add the spinach, toss for 2 more minutes and serve.

Nutrition (for 100g): 198 Calories 0.7g Fat 7g Carbohydrates 10g Protein 725mg Sodium

Basil and Tomato Soup

Preparation Time : 10 minutes

Cooking Time : 25 minutes

Servings : 2

Difficulty Level : Average

Ingredients:

- 2 tbsps. vegetable broth
- 1 minced garlic clove
- ½ c. white onion
- 1 chopped celery stalk
- 1 chopped carrot
- 3 c. tomatoes, chopped
- Salt and pepper
- 2 bay leaves
- 1 ½ c. unsweetened almond milk
- 1/3 c. basil leaves

Directions:

Cook the vegetable broth in a large saucepan over medium heat. Add in garlic and onions and cook for 4 minutes. Add in carrots and celery. Cook for 1 more minute.

Put in the tomatoes and bring to a boil. Simmer for 15 minutes. Add the almond milk, basil and bay leaves. Season it and serve.

Nutrition (for 100g): 213 Calories 3.9g Fat 9g Carbohydrates 11g Protein 817mg Sodium

Butternut Squash Hummus

Preparation Time : 10 minutes

Cooking Time : 15 minutes

Servings : 4

Difficulty Level : Easy

Ingredients:

- 2 lbs. or 900 g seeded butternut squash, peeled
- 1 tbsp. olive oil
- ¼ c. tahini
- 2 tbsps. lemon juice
- 2 minced cloves garlic
- Salt and pepper

Directions:

Heat the oven to 300 F/148 C. Coat the butternut squash with olive oil. Set in a baking dish to bake for 15 minutes in the oven. When the squash is cooked, incorporate in a food processor together with the rest of the ingredients.

Pulse until smooth. Serve with carrots and celery sticks. For further use of place in individual containers, put a label and store it in the fridge. Allow warming at room temperature before heating in the microwave oven.

Nutrition (for 100g): 115 Calories 5.8g Fat 6.7g Carbohydrates 10g Protein 946mg Sodium

Ham Muffins

Preparation Time : 10 minutes
Cooking Time : 15 minutes
Servings : 6
Difficulty Level : Average

Ingredients:

- 9 ham slices
- 1/3 c. chopped spinach
- ¼ c. crumbled feta cheese
- ½ c. chopped roasted red peppers
- Salt and black pepper
- 1½ tbsps. basil pesto
- 5 whisked eggs

Directions:

Grease a muffin tin. Use 1 ½ ham slices to line each of the muffin molds. Except for black pepper, salt, pesto, and eggs, divide the rest of the ingredients into your ham cups. Using a bowl, whisk together the pepper, salt, pesto, and eggs. Pour your pepper mixture on top. Set oven to 400 F/204 C and bake for about 15 minutes. Serve immediately.

Nutrition (for 100g): 109 Calories 6.7g Fat 1.8g Carbohydrates 9g Protein 386mg Sodium

Farro Salad

Preparation Time : 10 minutes
Cooking Time : 0 minutes
Servings : 2
Difficulty Level : Easy

Ingredients:

- 1 tbsp. olive oil
- Salt and black pepper
- 1 bunch baby spinach, chopped
- 1 pitted avocado, peeled and chopped
- 1 minced garlic clove
- 2 c. cooked farro
- ½ c. cherry tomatoes, cubed

Directions:

Adjust your heat to medium. Set oil in a pan and heat. Toss in the rest of the ingredients. Cook the mixture for approximately 5 minutes. Set in serving plates and enjoy.

Nutrition (for 100g): 157 Calories 13.7g Fat 5.5g Carbohydrates 6g Protein 615mg Sodium

Cranberry and Dates Squares

Preparation Time : 10 minutes

Cooking Time : 20 minutes

Servings : 10

Difficulty Level : Easy

Ingredients:

- 12 pitted dates, chopped
- 1 tsp. vanilla extract
- ¼ c. honey
- ½ c. rolled oats
- ¾ c. dried cranberries
- ¼ c. melted almond avocado oil
- 1 c. chopped walnuts, roasted
- ¼ c. pumpkin seeds

Directions:

Using a bowl, stir in all ingredients to mix.

Line a parchment paper on a baking sheet. Press the mixture on the setup. Set in your freezer for about 30 minutes. Slice into 10 squares and enjoy.

Nutrition (for 100g): 263 Calories 13.4g Fat 14.3g Carbohydrates 7g Protein 845mg Sodium

Lentils and Cheddar Frittata

Preparation Time : 5 minutes

Cooking Time : 17 minutes

Servings : 4

Difficulty Level : Easy

Ingredients:

- 1 chopped red onion
- 2 tbsps. olive oil
- 1 c. boiled sweet potatoes, chopped
- ¾ c. chopped ham
- 4 whisked eggs
- ¾ c. cooked lentils
- 2 tbsps. Greek yogurt
- Salt and black pepper
- ½ c. halved cherry tomatoes,
- ¾ c. grated cheddar cheese

Directions:

Adjust your heat to medium and set a pan in place. Add in oil to heat. Stir in onion and allow to sauté for about 2 minutes. Except for cheese and eggs, toss in the other ingredients and cook for 3 more minutes. Add in the eggs, top with cheese. Cook for 10 more minutes while covered.

Slice the frittata, set in serving bowls and enjoy.

Nutrition (for 100g): 274 Calories 17.3g Fat 3.5g Carbohydrates 6g Protein 843mg Sodium

Tuna Sandwich

Preparation Time : 5 minutes

Cooking Time : 5 minutes

Servings : 2

Difficulty Level : Easy

Ingredients:

- 6 oz. or 170 g canned tuna, drained and flaked
- 1 pitted avocado, peeled and mashed
- 4 whole-wheat bread slices
- Pinch salt and black pepper
- 1 tbsp. crumbled feta cheese
- 1 c. baby spinach

Directions:

Using a bowl, stir in pepper, salt, tuna, and cheese to mix. To the bread slices, apply a spread of the mashed avocado.

Equally, divide the tuna mixture and spinach onto 2 of the slices. Top with the remaining 2 slices. Serve.

Nutrition (for 100g): 283 Calories 11.2g Fat 3.4g Carbohydrates 8g Protein 754mg Sodium

Spelled Salad

Preparation Time : 15 minutes

Cooking Time : 30 minutes

Servings : 4

Difficulty Level : Average

Ingredients:

- <u>Salad</u>
- 2 ½ cups of vegetable broth
- ¾ cup of crumbled feta cheese
- 1 can chickpeas, drained
- 1 cucumber, chopped
- 1 ½ cup pearl spelled
- 1 tablespoon of olive oil
- ½ sliced onion
- 2 cups of baby spinach, chopped
- 1 pint of cherry tomatoes
- 1 ¼ cups of water
- <u>Dressing:</u>
- 2 tablespoons of lemon juice
- 1 tablespoon of honey
- ¼ cup olive oil
- ¼ tsp oregano
- 1 pinch of red pepper flakes
- ¼ teaspoon of salt

- 1 tablespoon of red wine vinegar

Directions:

Heat the oil in a skillet. Add the spelled and cook for a minute. Be sure to stir it regularly during cooking. Fill in water and broth, then bring to a boil. Reduce the heat and simmer until the spelled is tender, about 30 minutes. Drain the water and transfer the spelled to a bowl.

Add the spinach and mix. Let cool for about 20 minutes. Add the cucumber, onions, tomatoes, peppers, chickpeas and feta. Mix well to get a good mixture. Step back and prepare the dressing.

Mix all the dressing ingredients and mix well until smooth. Pour it into the bowl and mix it well. Season well to taste.

Nutrition (for 100g): 365 Calories 10g Fat 43g Carbohydrates 13g Protein 845mg Sodium

Chickpea and Zucchini Salad

Preparation Time : 10 minutes
Cooking Time : 0 minutes
Servings : 3
Difficulty Level : Easy

Ingredients:

- ¼ cup balsamic vinegar
- 1/3 cup chopped basil leaves
- 1 tablespoon of capers, drained and chopped
- ½ cup crumbled feta cheese
- 1 can chickpeas, drained
- 1 garlic clove, chopped
- ½ cup Kalamata olives, chopped
- 1/3 cup of olive oil
- ½ cup sweet onion, chopped
- ½ tsp oregano
- 1 pinch of red pepper flakes, crushed
- ¾ cup red bell pepper, chopped
- 1 tablespoon chopped rosemary
- 2 cups of zucchini, diced
- salt and pepper, to taste

Directions:

Combine the vegetables in a bowl and cover well.

Serve at room temperature. But for best results, refrigerate the bowl for a few hours before serving, to allow the flavors to blend.

Nutrition (for 100g): 258 Calories 12g Fat 19g Carbohydrates 5.6g Protein 686mg Sodium

Provencal Artichoke Salad

Preparation Time : 15 minutes

Cooking Time : 5 minutes

Servings : 3

Difficulty Level : Easy

Ingredients:

- 9 oz artichoke hearts
- 1 teaspoon of chopped basil
- 2 garlic cloves, chopped
- 1 lemon zest
- 1 tablespoon olives, chopped
- 1 tablespoon of olive oil
- ½ chopped onion
- 1 pinch, ½ teaspoon of salt
- 2 tomatoes, chopped
- 3 tablespoons of water
- ½ glass of white wine
- salt and pepper, to taste

Directions:

Heat the oil in a skillet. Sauté the onion and garlic. Cook until the onions are translucent and season with a pinch of salt. Pour in the white wine and simmer until the wine is reduced by half.

Add the chopped tomatoes, artichoke hearts and water. Simmer then add the lemon zest and about ½ teaspoon of salt. Cover and cook for about 6 minutes.

Add the olives and basil. Season well and enjoy!

Nutrition (for 100g): 147 Calories 13g Fat 18g Carbohydrates 4g Protein 689mg Sodium

Bulgarian Salad

Preparation Time : 10 minutes

Cooking Time : 20 minutes

Servings : 2

Difficulty Level : Average

Ingredients:

- 2 cups of bulgur
- 1 tablespoon of butter
- 1 cucumber, cut into pieces
- ¼ cup dill
- ¼ cup black olives, cut in half
- 1 tablespoon, 2 teaspoons of olive oil
- 4 cups of water
- 2 teaspoons of red wine vinegar
- salt, to taste

Directions:

In a saucepan, toast the bulgur on a mixture of butter and olive oil. Leave to cook until the bulgur is golden brown and begins to crack.

Add water and season with salt. Wrap everything and simmer for about 20 minutes or until the bulgur is tender.

In a bowl, mix the cucumber pieces with the olive oil, dill, red wine vinegar and black olives. Mix everything well.

It combines cucumber and bulgur.

Nutrition (for 100g): 386 Calories 14g Fat 55g Carbohydrates 9g Protein 545mg Sodium

Falafel Salad Bowl

Preparation Time : 15 minutes
Cooking Time : 5 minutes
Servings : 2
Difficulty Level : Easy

Ingredients:

- 1 tablespoon of chili garlic sauce
- 1 tablespoon of garlic and dill sauce
- 1 pack of vegetarian falafels
- 1 box of humus
- 2 tablespoons of lemon juice
- 1 tablespoon of pitted kalamata olives
- 1 tablespoon of extra virgin olive oil
- ¼ cup onion, diced
- 2 cups of chopped parsley
- 2 cups of crisp pita
- 1 pinch of salt
- 1 tablespoon of tahini sauce
- ½ cup diced tomato

Directions:

Cook the prepared falafels. Put it aside. Prepare the salad. Mix the parsley, onion, tomato, lemon juice, olive oil and salt. Throw it all out and put everything aside. Transfer everything to the serving bowls. Add the parsley and cover with humus and falafel. Sprinkle bowl with tahini sauce, chili garlic sauce and dill sauce. Upon serving, add the lemon juice and mix the salad well. Serve with pita bread on the side.

Nutrition (for 100g): 561 Calories 11g Fat 60.1g Carbohydrates 18.5g Protein 944mg Sodium

Easy Greek Salad

Preparation Time : 15 minutes

Cooking Time : 0 minutes

Servings : 2

Difficulty Level : Easy

Ingredients:

- 4 oz Greek feta cheese, cubed
- 5 cucumbers, cut lengthwise
- 1 teaspoon of honey
- 1 lemon, chewed and grated
- 1 cup kalamata olives, pitted and halved
- ¼ cup extra virgin olive oil
- 1 onion, sliced
- 1 teaspoon of oregano
- 1 pinch of fresh oregano (for garnish)
- 12 tomatoes, quartered
- ¼ cup red wine vinegar
- salt and pepper, to taste

Directions:

In a bowl, soak the onions in salted water for 15 minutes. In a large bowl, combine the honey, lemon juice, lemon peel, oregano, salt and pepper. Mix everything. Gradually add the olive oil, beating as you do, until the oil emulsifies. Add the olives and tomatoes. Put it right. Add the cucumbers

Drain the onions soaked in salted water and add them to the salad mixture. Top the salad with fresh oregano and feta. Dash with olive oil and season with pepper, to taste.

Nutrition (for 100g): 292 Calories 17g Fat 12g Carbohydrates 6g Protein 743mg Sodium

Arugula Salad with Figs and Walnuts

Preparation Time : 15 minutes

Cooking Time : 10 minutes

Servings : 2

Difficulty Level : Easy

Ingredients:

- 5 oz arugula
- 1 carrot, scraped
- 1/8 teaspoon of cayenne pepper
- 3 oz of goat cheese, crumbled
- 1 can salt-free chickpeas, drained
- ½ cup dried figs, cut into wedges
- 1 teaspoon of honey
- 3 tablespoons of olive oil
- 2 teaspoons of balsamic vinegar
- ½ walnuts cut in half
- salt, to taste

Directions:

Preheat the oven to 175 degrees. In a baking dish, combine the nuts, 1 tablespoon of olive oil, cayenne pepper and 1/8 teaspoon of salt. Transfer the baking sheet in the oven and bake it until the nuts are golden. Set it aside when you are done.

In a bowl, incorporate the honey, balsamic vinegar, 2 tablespoons of oil and ¾ teaspoon of salt.

In a large bowl, combine the arugula, carrot and figs. Add nuts and goat cheese and drizzle with balsamic honey vinaigrette. Make sure you cover everything.

Nutrition (for 100g): 403 Calories 9g Fat 35g Carbohydrates 13g Protein 844mg Sodium

Cauliflower Salad with Tahini Vinaigrette

Preparation Time : 15 minutes
Cooking Time : 5 minutes
Servings : 2
Difficulty Level : Average

Ingredients:

- 1 ½ lb. of cauliflower
- ¼ cup of dried cherries
- 3 tablespoons of lemon juice
- 1 tablespoon of fresh mint, chopped
- 1 teaspoon of olive oil
- ½ cup chopped parsley
- 3 tablespoons of roasted salted pistachios, chopped
- ½ teaspoon of salt
- ¼ Cup of shallot, chopped
- 2 tablespoons of tahini

Directions:

Grate the cauliflower in a microwave-safe container Add olive oil and ¼ salt. Be sure to cover and season the cauliflower evenly. Wrap the bowl with plastic wrap and heat it in the microwave for about 3 minutes.

Put the rice with the cauliflower on a baking sheet and let cool for about 10 minutes. Add the lemon juice and the shallots. Let it rest to allow the cauliflower to absorb the flavor.

Add the mixture of tahini, cherries, parsley, mint and salt. Mix everything well. Sprinkle with roasted pistachios before serving.

Nutrition (for 100g): 165 Calories 10g Fat 20g Carbohydrates 6g Protein 651mg Sodium

Mediterranean Potato Salad

Preparation Time : 15 minutes

Cooking Time : 10 minutes

Servings : 2

Difficulty Level : Easy

Ingredients:

- 1 bunch of basil leaves, torn
- 1 garlic clove, crushed
- 1 tablespoon of olive oil
- 1 onion, sliced
- 1 teaspoon of oregano
- 100 g of roasted red pepper. Slices
- 300g potatoes, cut in half
- 1 can of cherry tomatoes
- salt and pepper, to taste

Directions:

Sauté the onions in a saucepan. Add oregano and garlic. He cooks everything for a minute. Add the pepper and tomatoes. Season well, then simmer for about 10 minutes. Put that aside.

In a saucepan, boil the potatoes in salted water. Cook until tender, about 15 minutes. Drain well. Mix the potatoes with the sauce and add the basil and olives. Finally, throw everything away before serving.

Nutrition (for 100g): 111 Calories 9g Fat 16g Carbohydrates 3g Protein 745mg Sodium

Quinoa and Pistachio Salad

Preparation Time : 10 minutes

Cooking Time : 15 minutes

Servings : 2

Difficulty Level : Easy

Ingredients:

- ¼ teaspoon of cumin
- ½ cup of dried currants
- 1 teaspoon grated lemon zest
- 2 tablespoons of lemon juice
- ½ cup green onions, chopped
- 1 tablespoon of chopped mint
- 2 tablespoons of extra virgin olive oil
- ¼ cup chopped parsley
- ¼ teaspoon ground pepper
- 1/3 cup pistachios, chopped
- 1 ¼ cups uncooked quinoa
- 1 2/3 cup of water

Directions:

In a saucepan, combine 1 2/3 cups of water, raisins and quinoa. Cook everything until boiling then reduce the heat. Simmer everything for about 10 minutes and let the quinoa become frothy. Set it aside for about 5 minutes. In a container, transfer the quinoa mixture. Add the nuts, mint, onions and parsley. Mix everything. In separate bowl, incorporate the lemon zest, lemon juice, currants, cumin and oil. Beat them together. Mix the dry and wet ingredients.

Nutrition (for 100g): 248 Calories 8g Fat 35g Carbohydrates 7g Protein 914mg Sodium

Cucumber Chicken Salad with Spicy Peanut Dressing

Preparation Time : 15 minutes
Cooking Time : 0 minutes
Servings : 2
Difficulty Level : Average

Ingredients:

- 1/2 cup peanut butter
- 1 tablespoon sambal oelek (chili paste)
- 1 tablespoon low-sodium soy sauce
- 1 teaspoon grilled sesame oil
- 4 tablespoons of water, or more if necessary
- 1 cucumber with peeled and cut into thin strips
- 1 cooked chicken fillet, grated into thin strips
- 2 tablespoons chopped peanuts

Directions:

Combine peanut butter, soy sauce, sesame oil, sambal oelek, and water in a bowl. Place the cucumber slices on a dish. Garnish with grated chicken and sprinkle with sauce. Sprinkle the chopped peanuts.

Nutrition (for 100g): 720 calories 54 g fat 8.9g carbohydrates 45.9g protein 733mg sodium

German Hot Potato Salad

Preparation Time : 10 minutes

Cooking Time : 30 minutes

Servings : 12

Difficulty Level : Average

Ingredients:

- 9 peeled potatoes
- 6 slices of bacon
- 1/8 teaspoon ground black pepper
- 1/2 teaspoon celery seed
- 2 tablespoons white sugar
- 2 teaspoons salt
- 3/4 cup water
- 1/3 cup distilled white vinegar
- 2 tablespoons all-purpose flour
- 3/4 cup chopped onions

Directions:

Boil salted water in a large pot. Put in the potatoes and cook until soft but still firm, about 30 minutes. Drain, let cool and cut finely. Over medium heat, cook bacon in a pan. Drain, crumble and set aside. Save the cooking juices. Cook onions in bacon grease until golden brown.

Combine flour, sugar, salt, celery seed, and pepper in a small bowl. Add sautéed onions and cook, stirring until bubbling, and remove from heat. Stir in the water and vinegar, then bring back to the fire and bring to a boil, stirring constantly. Boil and stir. Slowly add bacon and potato slices to the vinegar/water mixture, stirring gently until the potatoes are warmed up.

Nutrition (for 100g): 205 calories 6.5g fat 32.9g carbohydrates 4.3g protein 814mg sodium

Chicken Fiesta Salad

Preparation Time : 20 minutes

Cooking Time : 20 minutes

Servings : 4

Difficulty Level : Easy

Ingredients:

- 2 halves of chicken fillet without skin or bones
- 1 packet of herbs for fajitas, divided
- 1 tablespoon vegetable oil
- 1 can black beans, rinsed and drained
- 1 box of Mexican-style corn
- 1/2 cup of salsa
- 1 packet of green salad
- 1 onion, minced
- 1 tomato, quartered

Directions:

Rub the chicken evenly with 1/2 of the herbs for fajitas. Cook the oil in a frying pan over medium heat and cook the chicken for 8 minutes on the side by side or until the juice is clear; put aside. Combine beans, corn, salsa, and other 1/2 fajita spices in a large pan. Heat over medium heat until lukewarm. Prepare the salad by mixing green vegetables, onion, and tomato. Cover the chicken salad and dress the beans and corn mixture.

Nutrition (for 100g): 311 calories 6.4g fat 42.2g carbohydrates 23g protein 853mg sodium

Corn & Black Bean Salad

Preparation Time : 10 minutes

Cooking Time : 0 minutes

Servings : 4

Difficulty Level : Easy

Ingredients:

- 2 tablespoons vegetable oil
- 1/4 cup balsamic vinegar
- 1/2 teaspoon of salt
- 1/2 teaspoon of white sugar
- 1/2 teaspoon ground cumin
- 1/2 teaspoon ground black pepper
- 1/2 teaspoon chili powder
- 3 tablespoons chopped fresh coriander
- 1 can black beans (15 oz)
- 1 can of sweetened corn (8.75 oz) drained

Directions:

Combine balsamic vinegar, oil, salt, sugar, black pepper, cumin and chili powder in a small bowl. Combine black corn and beans in a medium bowl. Mix with vinegar and oil vinaigrette and garnish with coriander. Cover and refrigerate overnight.

Nutrition (for 100g): 214 calories 8.4 g fat 28.6g carbohydrates 7.5g protein 415mg sodium

Awesome Pasta Salad

Preparation Time : 30 minutes

Cooking Time : 10 minutes

Servings : 16

Difficulty Level : Average

Ingredients:

- 1 (16-oz) fusilli pasta package
- 3 cups of cherry tomatoes
- 1/2 pound of provolone, diced
- 1/2 pound of sausage, diced
- 1/4 pound of pepperoni, cut in half
- 1 large green pepper
- 1 can of black olives, drained
- 1 jar of chilis, drained
- 1 bottle (8 oz) Italian vinaigrette

Directions:

Boil a lightly salted water in a pot. Stir in the pasta and cook for about 8 to 10 minutes or until al dente. Drain and rinse with cold water.

Combine pasta with tomatoes, cheese, salami, pepperoni, green pepper, olives, and peppers in a large bowl. Pour the vinaigrette and mix well.

Nutrition (for 100g): 310 calories 17.7g fat 25.9g carbohydrates 12.9g protein 746mg sodium

Tuna Salad

Preparation Time : 20 minutes

Cooking Time : 0 minutes

Servings : 4

Difficulty Level : Easy

Ingredients:

- 1 (19 ounce) can of garbanzo beans
- 2 tablespoons mayonnaise
- 2 teaspoons of spicy brown mustard
- 1 tablespoon sweet pickle
- Salt and pepper to taste
- 2 chopped green onions

Directions:

Combine green beans, mayonnaise, mustard, sauce, chopped green onions, salt and pepper in a medium bowl. Mix well.

Nutrition (for 100g): 220 calories 7.2g fat 32.7g carbohydrates 7g protein 478mg sodium

Southern Potato Salad

Preparation Time : 15 minutes

Cooking Time : 15 minutes

Servings : 4

Difficulty Level : Average

Ingredients:

- 4 potatoes
- 4 eggs
- 1/2 stalk of celery, finely chopped
- 1/4 cup sweet taste
- 1 clove of garlic minced
- 2 tablespoons mustard
- 1/2 cup mayonnaise
- salt and pepper to taste

Directions:

Boil water in a pot then situate the potatoes and cook until soft but still firm, about 15 minutes; drain and chop. Transfer the eggs in a pan and cover with cold water.

Boil the water; cover, remove from heat, and let the eggs soak in hot water for 10 minutes. Remove then shell and chop.

Combine potatoes, eggs, celery, sweet sauce, garlic, mustard, mayonnaise, salt, and pepper in a large bowl. Mix and serve hot.

Nutrition (for 100g): 460 calories 27.4g fat 44.6g carbohydrates 11.3g protein 214mg sodium

Seven-Layer Salad

Preparation Time : 15 minutes

Cooking Time : 5 minutes

Servings : 10

Difficulty Level : Average

Ingredients:

- 1-pound bacon
- 1 head iceberg lettuce
- 1 red onion, minced
- 1 pack of 10 frozen peas, thawed
- 10 oz grated cheddar cheese
- 1 cup chopped cauliflower
- 1 1/4 cup mayonnaise
- 2 tablespoons white sugar
- 2/3 cup grated Parmesan cheese

Directions:

Put the bacon in a huge, shallow frying pan. Bake over medium heat until smooth. Crumble and set aside. Situate the chopped lettuce in a large bowl and cover with a layer of an onion, peas, grated cheese, cauliflower, and bacon.

Prepare the vinaigrette by mixing the mayonnaise, sugar, and parmesan cheese. Pour over the salad and cool to cool.

Nutrition (for 100g): 387 calories 32.7g fat 9.9g carbohydrates 14.5g protein 609mg sodium

Kale, Quinoa & Avocado Salad with Lemon Dijon Vinaigrette

Preparation Time : 5 minutes
Cooking Time : 25 minutes
Servings : 4
Difficulty Level : Difficult

Ingredients:

- 2/3 cup of quinoa
- 1 1/3 cup of water
- 1 bunch of kale, torn into bite-sized pieces
- 1/2 avocado - peeled, diced and pitted
- 1/2 cup chopped cucumber
- 1/3 cup chopped red pepper
- 2 tablespoons chopped red onion
- 1 tablespoon of feta crumbled

Directions:

Boil the quinoa and 1 1/3 cup of water in a pan. Adjust heat and simmer until quinoa is tender and water is absorbed for about 15 to 20 minutes. Set aside to cool.

Place the cabbage in a steam basket over more than an inch of boiling water in a pan. Seal the pan with a lid and steam until hot, about 45 seconds; transfer to a large plate. Garnish with cabbage, quinoa, avocado, cucumber, pepper, red onion, and feta cheese.

Combine olive oil, lemon juice, Dijon mustard, sea salt, and black pepper in a bowl until the oil is emulsified in the dressing; pour over the salad.

Nutrition (for 100g): 342 calories 20.3g fat 35.4g carbohydrates 8.9g protein 705mg sodium

Chicken Salad

Preparation Time : 20 minutes
Cooking Time : 0 minutes
Servings : 9
Difficulty Level : Easy

Ingredients:

- 1/2 cup mayonnaise
- 1/2 teaspoon of salt
- 3/4 teaspoon of poultry herbs
- 1 tablespoon lemon juice
- 3 cups cooked chicken breast, diced
- 1/4 teaspoon ground black pepper
- 1/4 teaspoon garlic powder
- 1/4 teaspoon onion powder
- 1/2 cup finely chopped celery
- 1 (8 oz) box of water chestnuts, drained and chopped
- 1/2 cup chopped green onions
- 1 1/2 cups green grapes cut in half
- 1 1/2 cups diced Swiss cheese

Directions:

Combine mayonnaise, salt, chicken spices, onion powder, garlic powder, pepper, and lemon juice in a medium bowl. Combine chicken, celery, green onions, water chestnuts, Swiss cheese, and raisins in a big bowl. Stir in the mayonnaise mixture and coat. Cool until ready to serve.

Nutrition (for 100g): 293 calories 19.5g fat 10.3g carbohydrates 19.4g protein 454mg sodium

Cobb Salad

Preparation Time : 5 minutes

Cooking Time : 15 minutes

Servings : 6

Difficulty Level : Difficult

Ingredients:

- 6 slices of bacon
- 3 eggs
- 1 cup Iceberg lettuce, grated
- 3 cups cooked minced chicken meat
- 2 tomatoes, seeded and minced
- 3/4 cup of blue cheese, crumbled
- 1 avocado - peeled, pitted and diced
- 3 green onions, minced
- 1 bottle (8 oz.) Ranch Vinaigrette

Directions:

Situate the eggs in a pan and soak them completely with cold water. Boil the water. Cover and remove from heat and let the eggs rest in hot water for 10 to 12 minutes. Remove from hot water, let cool, peel, and chop. Situate the bacon in a big, deep frying pan. Bake over medium heat until smooth. Set aside.

Divide the grated lettuce into separate plates. Spread chicken, eggs, tomatoes, blue cheese, bacon, avocado, and green onions in rows on lettuce. Sprinkle with your favorite vinaigrette and enjoy.

Nutrition (for 100g): 525 calories 39.9g fat 10.2g carbohydrates 31.7g protein 701mg sodium

Broccoli Salad

Preparation Time : 10 minutes

Cooking Time : 15 minutes

Servings : 6

Difficulty Level : Average

Ingredients:

- 10 slices of bacon
- 1 cup fresh broccoli
- ¼ cup red onion, minced
- ½ cup raisins
- 3 tablespoons white wine vinegar
- 2 tablespoons white sugar
- 1 cup mayonnaise
- 1 cup of sunflower seeds

Directions:

Cook the bacon in a deep-frying pan over medium heat. Drain, crumble, and set aside. Combine broccoli, onion, and raisins in a medium bowl. Mix vinegar, sugar, and mayonnaise in a small bowl. Pour over the broccoli mixture and mix. Cool for at least two hours.

Before serving, mix the salad with crumbled bacon and sunflower seeds.

Nutrition (for 100g): 559 calories 48.1g fat 31g carbohydrates 18g protein 584mg sodium

Strawberry Spinach Salad

Preparation Time : 10 minutes

Cooking Time : 0 minutes

Servings : 4

Difficulty Level : Easy

Ingredients:

- 2 tablespoons sesame seeds
- 1 tablespoon poppy seeds
- 1/2 cup white sugar
- 1/2 cup olive oil
- 1/4 cup distilled white vinegar
- 1/4 teaspoon paprika
- 1/4 teaspoon Worcestershire sauce
- 1 tablespoon minced onion
- 10 ounces fresh spinach
- 1-quart strawberries - cleaned, hulled and sliced
- 1/4 cup almonds, blanched and slivered

Directions:

In a medium bowl, whisk together the same seeds, poppy seeds, sugar, olive oil, vinegar, paprika, Worcestershire sauce, and onion. Cover, and chill for one hour.

In a large bowl, incorporate the spinach, strawberries, and almonds. Drizzle dressing over salad and toss. Refrigerate 10 to 15 minutes before serving.

Nutrition (for 100g): 491 calories 35.2g fat 42.9g carbohydrates 6g protein 691mg sodium

Pear Salad with Roquefort Cheese

Preparation Time : 20 minutes

Cooking Time : 10 minutes

Servings : 2

Difficulty Level : Average

Ingredients:

- 1 leaf lettuce, torn into bite-sized pieces
- 3 pears - peeled, cored and diced
- 5 ounces Roquefort, crumbled
- 1 avocado - peeled, seeded and diced
- 1/2 cup chopped green onions
- 1/4 cup white sugar
- 1/2 cup pecan nuts
- 1/3 cup olive oil
- 3 tablespoons red wine vinegar
- 1 1/2 teaspoon of white sugar
- 1 1/2 teaspoon of prepared mustard
- 1/2 teaspoon of salted black pepper
- 1 clove of garlic

Directions:

Stir in 1/4 cup of sugar with the pecans in a pan over medium heat. Continue to stir gently until the sugar caramelized with pecans. Cautiously transfer the nuts to wax paper. Let it chill and break into pieces.

Mix for vinaigrette oil, marinade, 1 1/2 teaspoon of sugar, mustard, chopped garlic, salt, and pepper.

In a deep bowl, combine lettuce, pears, blue cheese, avocado, and green onions. Put vinaigrette over salad, sprinkle with pecans and serve.

Nutrition (for 100g): 426 calories 31.6g fat 33.1g carbohydrates 8g protein 481mg sodium

Mexican Bean Salad

Preparation Time : 15 minutes
Cooking Time : 0 minutes
Servings : 6
Difficulty Level : Easy

Ingredients:

- 1 can black beans (15 oz), drained
- 1 can red beans (15 oz), drained
- 1 can white beans (15 oz), drained
- 1 green pepper, minced
- 1 red pepper, minced
- 1 pack of frozen corn kernels
- 1 red onion, minced
- 2 tablespoons fresh lime juice
- 1/2 cup olive oil
- 1/2 cup red wine vinegar
- 1 tablespoon lemon juice
- 1 tablespoon salt
- 2 tablespoons white sugar
- 1 clove of crushed garlic
- 1/4 cup chopped coriander
- 1/2 tablespoon ground cumin
- 1/2 tablespoon ground black pepper
- 1 dash of hot pepper sauce

- 1/2 teaspoon chili powder

Directions:

Combine beans, peppers, frozen corn, and red onion in a large bowl. Combine olive oil, lime juice, red wine vinegar, lemon juice, sugar, salt, garlic, coriander, cumin, and black pepper in a small bowl — season with hot sauce and chili powder.

Pour the vinaigrette with olive oil over the vegetables; mix well. Cool well and serve cold.

Nutrition (for 100g): 334 calories 14.8g fat 41.7g carbohydrates 11.2g protein 581mg sodium

Melon Salad

Preparation Time : 20 minutes
Cooking Time : 0 minutes
Servings : 6
Difficulty Level : Average

Ingredients:

- ¼ teaspoon sea salt
- ¼ teaspoon black pepper
- 1 tablespoon balsamic vinegar
- 1 cantaloupe, quartered & seeded
- 12 watermelon, small & seedless
- 2 cups mozzarella balls, fresh
- 1/3 cup basil, fresh & torn
- 2 tbsp. olive oil

Directions:

Scrape out balls of cantaloupe, and the place them in a colander over a serving bowl. Use your melon baller to cut the watermelon as well, and then put them in with your cantaloupe.

Allow your fruit to drain for ten minutes, and then refrigerate the juice for another recipe. It can even be added to smoothies. Wipe the bowl dry, and then place your fruit in it.

Add in your basil, oil, vinegar, mozzarella and tomatoes before seasoning with salt and pepper. Gently mix and serve immediately or chilled.

Nutrition (for 100g): 218 Calories 13g Fat 9g Carbohydrates 10g Protein 581mg Sodium

Orange Celery Salad

Preparation Time : 15 minutes

Cooking Time : 0 minutes

Servings : 6

Difficulty Level : Easy

Ingredients:

- 1 tablespoon lemon juice, fresh
- ¼ teaspoon sea salt, fine
- ¼ teaspoon black pepper
- 1 tablespoon olive brine
- 1 tablespoon olive oil
- ¼ cup red onion, sliced
- ½ cup green olives
- 2 oranges, peeled & sliced
- 3 celery stalks, sliced diagonally in ½ inch slices

Directions:

Put your oranges, olives, onion and celery in a shallow bowl. In a different bowl whisk your oil, olive brine and lemon juice, pour this over your salad. Season with salt and pepper before serving.

Nutrition (for 100g): 65 Calories 7g Fats 9g Carbohydrates 2g Protein 614mg Sodium

Roasted Broccoli Salad

Preparation Time : 20 minutes

Cooking Time : 10 minutes

Servings : 4

Difficulty Level : Difficult

Ingredients:

- 1 lb. broccoli, cut into florets & stem sliced
- 3 tablespoons olive oil, divided
- 1-pint cherry tomatoes
- 1 ½ teaspoons honey, raw & divided
- 3 cups cubed bread, whole grain
- 1 tablespoon balsamic vinegar
- ½ teaspoon black pepper
- ¼ teaspoon sea salt, fine
- grated parmesan for serving

Directions:

Prepare oven at 450 degrees, and then get out a rimmed baking sheet. Place it in the oven to heat up. Drizzle your broccoli with a tablespoon of oil, and toss to coat.

Remove the baking sheet form the oven, and spoon the broccoli on it. Leave oil it eh bottom of the bowl, add in your tomatoes, toss to coat, and then toss your tomatoes with a tablespoon of honey. Pour them on the same baking sheet as your broccoli.

Roast for fifteen minutes, and stir halfway through your cooking time. Add in your bread, and then roast for three more minutes. Whisk two tablespoons of oil, vinegar, and remaining honey. Season with salt and pepper. Pour this over your broccoli mix to serve.

Nutrition (for 100g): 226 Calories 12g Fat 26g Carbohydrates 7g Protein 581mg Sodium

Tomato Salad

Preparation Time : 20 minutes

Cooking Time : 0 minutes

Servings : 4

Difficulty Level : Easy

Ingredients:

- 1 cucumber, sliced
- ¼ cup sun dried tomatoes, chopped
- 1 lb. tomatoes, cubed
- ½ cup black olives
- 1 red onion, sliced
- 1 tablespoon balsamic vinegar
- ¼ cup parsley, fresh & chopped
- 2 tablespoons olive oil
- sea salt & black pepper to taste

Directions:

Get out a bowl and combine all of your vegetables together. To make your dressing mix all your seasoning, olive oil and vinegar. Toss with your salad and serve fresh.

Nutrition (for 100g): 126 Calories 9.2g Fat 11.5g Carbohydrates 2.1g Protein 681mg Sodium

Feta Beet Salad

Preparation Time : 15 minutes

Cooking Time : 0 minutes

Servings : 4

Difficulty Level : Easy

Ingredients:

- 6 red beets, cooked & peeled
- 3 ounces feta cheese, cubed
- 2 tablespoons olive oil
- 2 tablespoons balsamic vinegar

Directions:

Combine everything together, and then serve.

Nutrition (for 100g): 230 Calories 12g Fat 26.3g Carbohydrates 7.3g Protein 614mg Sodium

Cauliflower & Tomato Salad

Preparation Time : 15 minutes

Cooking Time : 0 minutes

Servings : 4

Difficulty Level : Easy

Ingredients:

- 1 head cauliflower, chopped
- 2 tablespoons parsley, fresh & chopped
- 2 cups cherry tomatoes, halved
- 2 tablespoons lemon juice, fresh
- 2 tablespoons pine nuts
- sea salt & black pepper to taste

Directions:

Mix your lemon juice, cherry tomatoes, cauliflower and parsley together, and then season. Top with pine nuts, and mix well before serving.

Nutrition (for 100g): 64 Calories 3.3g Fat 7.9g Carbohydrates 2.8g Protein 614mg Sodium

Pilaf with Cream Cheese

Preparation Time : 20 minutes

Cooking Time : 10 minutes

Servings : 6

Difficulty Level : Average

Ingredients:

- 2 cups yellow long grain rice, parboiled
- 1 cup onion
- 4 green onions
- 3 tablespoons butter
- 3 tablespoons vegetable broth
- 2 teaspoons cayenne pepper
- 1 teaspoon paprika
- ½ teaspoon cloves, minced
- 2 tablespoons mint leaves, fresh & chopped
- 1 bunch fresh mint leaves to garnish
- 1 tablespoons olive oil
- sea salt & black pepper to taste
- <u>Cheese Cream:</u>
- 3 tablespoons olive oil
- sea salt & black pepper to taste
- 9 ounces cream cheese

Directions:

Ready the oven at 360 degrees, and then pull out a pan. Heat your butter and olive oil together, and cook your onions and spring onions for two minutes.

Add in your salt, pepper, paprika, cloves, vegetable broth, rice and remaining seasoning. Sauté for three minutes. Wrap with foil, and bake for another half hour. Allow it to cool.

Mix in the cream cheese, cheese, olive oil, salt and pepper. Serve your pilaf garnished with fresh mint leaves.

Nutrition (for 100g): 364 Calories 30g Fat 20g Carbohydrates 5g Protein 511mg Sodium

Roasted Eggplant Salad

Preparation Time : 10 minutes

Cooking Time : 20 minutes

Servings : 6

Difficulty Level : Easy

Ingredients:

- 1 red onion, sliced
- 2 tablespoons parsley, fresh & chopped
- 1 teaspoon thyme
- 2 cups cherry tomatoes, halved
- sea salt & black pepper to taste
- 1 teaspoon oregano
- 3 tablespoons olive oil
- 1 teaspoon basil
- 3 eggplants, peeled & cubed

Directions:

Start by heating your oven to 350. Season your eggplant with basil, salt, pepper, oregano, thyme and olive oil. Situate it on a baking tray, and bake for a half hour. Toss with your remaining ingredients before serving.

Nutrition (for 100g): 148 Calories 7.7g Fat 20.5g Carbohydrates 3.5g Protein 660mg Sodium

Roasted Veggies

Preparation Time : 5 minutes

Cooking Time : 15 minutes

Servings : 12

Difficulty Level : Easy

Ingredients:

- 6 cloves garlic
- 6 tablespoons olive oil
- 1 fennel bulb, diced
- 1 zucchini, diced
- 2 red bell peppers, diced
- 6 potatoes, large & diced
- 2 teaspoons sea salt
- ½ cup balsamic vinegar
- ¼ cup rosemary, chopped & fresh
- 2 teaspoons vegetable bouillon powder

Directions:

Start by heating your oven to 400. Put your potatoes, fennel, zucchini, garlic and fennel on a baking dish, drizzling with olive oil. Sprinkle with salt, bouillon powder, and rosemary. Mix well, and then bake at 450 for thirty to forty minutes. Mix your vinegar into the vegetables before serving.

Nutrition (for 100g): 675 Calories 21g Fat 112g Carbohydrates 13g Protein 718mg Sodium

Pistachio Arugula Salad

Preparation Time : 20 minutes

Cooking Time : 0 minutes

Servings : 6

Difficulty Level : Easy

Ingredients:

- 6 cups kale, chopped
- ¼ cup olive oil
- 2 tablespoons lemon juice, fresh
- ½ teaspoon smoked paprika
- 2 cups arugula
- 1/3 cup pistachios, unsalted & shelled
- 6 tablespoons parmesan cheese, grated

Directions:

Get out a salad bowl and combine your oil, lemon, smoked paprika and kale. Gently massage the leaves for half a minute. Your kale should be coated well. Gently mix your arugula and pistachios when ready to serve.

Nutrition (for 100g): 150 Calories 12g Fat 8g Carbohydrates 5g Protein 637mg Sodium

Parmesan Barley Risotto

Preparation Time : 10 minutes
Cooking Time : 20 minutes
Servings : 6
Difficulty Level : Difficult

Ingredients:

- 1 cup yellow onion, chopped
- 1 tablespoon olive oil
- 4 cups vegetable broth, low sodium
- 2 cups pearl barley, uncooked
- ½ cup dry white wine
- 1 cup parmesan cheese, grated fine & divided
- sea salt & black pepper to taste
- fresh chives, chopped for serving
- lemon wedges for serving

Directions:

Add your broth into a saucepan and bring it to a simmer over medium-high heat. Get out a stock pot and put it over medium-high heat as well. Heat your oil before adding in your onion. Cook for eight minutes and stir occasionally. Add in your barley and cook for two minutes more. Stir in your barley, cooking until it's toasted.

Pour in the wine, cooking for a minute more. Most of the liquid should have evaporated before adding in a cup of warm broth. Cook and stir for two minutes. Your liquid should be absorbed. Add in the remaining broth by the cup, and cook until ach cup is absorbed. It should take about two minutes each time.

Pull out from the heat, add half a cup of cheese, and top with remaining cheese, chives, and lemon wedges.

Nutrition (for 100g): 345 Calories 7g Fat 56g Carbohydrates 14g Protein 912mg Sodium

Seafood & Avocado Salad

Preparation Time : 10 minutes

Cooking Time : 0 minutes

Servings : 4

Difficulty Level : Easy

Ingredients:

- 2 lbs. salmon, cooked & chopped
- 2 lbs. shrimp, cooked & chopped
- 1 cup avocado, chopped
- 1 cup mayonnaise
- 4 tablespoons lime juice, fresh
- 2 cloves garlic
- 1 cup sour cream
- sea salt & black pepper to taste
- ½ red onion, minced
- 1 cup cucumber, chopped

Directions:

Start by getting out a bowl and combine your garlic, salt, pepper, onion, mayonnaise, sour cream and lime juice,

Get out a different bowl and mix together your salmon, shrimp, cucumber, and avocado.

Add the mayonnaise mixture to your shrimp, and then allow it to sit for twenty minutes in the fridge before serving.

Nutrition (for 100g): 394 Calories 30g Fat 3g Carbohydrates 27g Protein 815mg Sodium

Mediterranean Shrimp Salad

Preparation Time : 40 minutes

Cooking Time : 0 minutes

Servings : 6

Difficulty Level : Easy

Ingredients:

- 1 ½ lbs. shrimp, cleaned & cooked
- 2 celery stalks, fresh
- 1 onion
- 2 green onions
- 4 eggs, boiled
- 3 potatoes, cooked
- 3 tablespoons mayonnaise
- sea salt & black pepper to taste

Directions:

Start by slicing your potatoes and chopping your celery. Slice your eggs, and season. Mix everything together. Put your shrimp over the eggs, and then serve with onion and green onions.

Nutrition (for 100g): 207 Calories 6g Fat 15g Carbohydrates 17g Protein 664mg Sodium

Chickpea Pasta Salad

Preparation Time : 10 minutes

Cooking Time : 15 minutes

Servings : 6

Difficulty Level : Average

Ingredients:

- 2 tablespoons olive oil
- 16 ounces rotelle pasta
- ½ cup cured olives, chopped
- 2 tablespoons oregano, fresh & minced
- 2 tablespoons parsley, fresh & chopped
- 1 bunch green onions, chopped
- ¼ cup red wine vinegar
- 15 ounces canned garbanzo beans, drained & rinsed
- ½ cup parmesan cheese, grated
- sea salt & black pepper to taste

Directions:

Boil water and put the pasta al dente and follow per package instructions. Drain it and rinse it using cold water.

Get out a skillet and heat your olive oil over medium heat. Add in your scallions, chickpeas, parsley, oregano and olives. Decrease the heat, and sauté for twenty minutes more. Allow this mixture to cool.

Toss your chickpea mixture with your pasta and add in your grated cheese, salt, pepper and vinegar. Let it chill for four hours or overnight before serving.

Nutrition (for 100g): 424 Calories 10g Fat 69g Carbohydrates 16g Protein 714mg Sodium

Mediterranean Stir Fry

Preparation Time : 10 minutes

Cooking Time : 30 minutes

Servings : 4

Difficulty Level : Average

Ingredients:

- 2 zucchinis
- 1 onion
- ¼ teaspoon sea salt
- 2 cloves garlic
- 3 teaspoons olive oil, divided
- 1 lb. chicken breasts, boneless
- 1 cup quick cooking barley
- 2 cups water
- ¼ teaspoon black pepper
- 1 teaspoon oregano
- ¼ teaspoon red pepper flakes
- ½ teaspoon basil
- 2 plum tomatoes
- ½ cup Greek olives, pitted
- 1 tablespoons parsley, fresh

Directions:

Start by removing the skin from your chicken, and then chop it into smaller pieces. Chop the garlic and parsley, and then chop your olives, zucchini, tomatoes and onions. Get out a saucepan and bring your water to a boil. Mix in your barley, letting it simmer for eight to ten minutes.

Turn off heat. Let it rest for five minutes. Get out a skillet and add in two teaspoons of olive oil. Stir fry your chicken once it's hot, and then remove it from heat. Cook the onion in your remaining oil. Mix in your remaining ingredients, and cook for an additional three to five minutes. Serve warm.

Nutrition (for 100g): 337 Calories 8.6g Fat 32.3g Carbohydrates 31.7g Protein 517mg Sodium

Balsamic Cucumber Salad

Preparation Time : 15 minutes

Cooking Time : 0 minutes

Servings : 4

Difficulty Level : Easy

Ingredients:

- 2/3 large English cucumber, halved and sliced
- 2/3 medium red onion, halved and thinly sliced
- 5 1/2 tablespoons balsamic vinaigrette
- 1 1/3 cups grape tomatoes, halved
- 1/2 cup crumbled reduced-fat feta cheese

Directions:

In a big bowl, mix cucumber, tomatoes and onion. Add vinaigrette; toss to coating. Refrigerate, covered, till serving. Just prior to serving, stir in cheese. Serve with a slotted teaspoon.

Nutrition (for 100g): 250 calories 12g fats 15g carbohydrates 34g protein 633mg Sodium

Beef Kefta Patties with Cucumber Salad

Preparation Time : 10 minutes

Cooking Time : 15 minutes

Servings : 2

Difficulty Level : Difficult

Ingredients:

- cooking spray
- 1/2-pound ground sirloin
- 2 tablespoons plus 2 tablespoons chopped fresh flat-leaf parsley, divided
- 1 1/2 teaspoons chopped peeled fresh ginger
- 1 teaspoon ground coriander
- 2 tablespoons chopped fresh cilantro
- 1/4 teaspoon salt
- 1/2 teaspoon ground cumin
- 1/4 teaspoon ground cinnamon
- 1 cup thinly sliced English cucumbers
- 1 tablespoon rice vinegar
- 1/4 cup plain fat-free Greek yogurt
- 1 1/2 teaspoons fresh lemon juice
- 1/4 teaspoon freshly ground black pepper
- 1 (6-inch) pitas, quartered

Directions:

Warmth a grill skillet over medium-high warmth. Coat pan with cooking spray. Combine beef, 1/4 glass parsley, cilantro, and next 5 elements in a medium bowl. Divide combination into 4 the same portions, shaping each into a 1/2-inch-thick patty. Add patties to pan; cook both sides until desired degree of doneness.

Mix cucumber and vinegar in a medium bowl; throw well. Combine fat-free yogurt, remaining 2 tablespoons parsley, juice, and pepper in a little bowl; stir with a whisk. Set up 1 patty and 1/2 cup cucumber mixture on each of 4 china. Top each offering with about 2 tablespoons yogurt spices. Serve each with 2 pita wedges.

Nutrition (for 100g): 116 calories 5g fats 11g carbohydrates 28g protein 642mg sodium

Chicken and Cucumber Salad with Parsley Pesto

Preparation Time : 15 minutes

Cooking Time : 5 minutes

Servings : 8

Difficulty Level : Easy

Ingredients:

- 2 2/3 cups packed fresh flat-leaf parsley leaves
- 1 1/3 cups fresh baby spinach
- 1 1/2 tablespoons toasted pine nuts
- 1 1/2 tablespoons grated Parmesan cheese
- 2 1/2 tablespoons fresh lemon juice
- 1 1/3 teaspoons kosher salt
- 1/3 teaspoon black pepper
- 1 1/3 medium garlic cloves, smashed
- 2/3 cup extra-virgin olive oil
- 5 1/3 cups shredded rotisserie chicken (from 1 chicken)
- 2 2/3 cups cooked shelled edamame
- 1 1/2 cans 1 (15-oz.) unsalted chickpeas, drained and rinsed
- 1 1/3 cups chopped English cucumbers
- 5 1/3 cups loosely packed arugula

Directions:

Combine parsley, spinach, lemon juice, pine nuts, cheese, garlic, salt, and pepper in food processor; process about 1 minute. With processor running, add oil; process until smooth, about 1 minute.

Stir together chicken, edamame, chickpeas, and cucumber in a large bowl. Add pesto; toss to combine.

Place 2/3 cup arugula in each of 6 bowls; top each with 1 cup chicken salad mixture. Serve immediately.

Nutrition (for 100g): 116 calories 12g fats 3g carbohydrates 9g protein 663mg sodium

Easy Arugula Salad

Preparation Time : 15 minutes

Cooking Time : 0 minutes

Servings : 6

Difficulty Level : Easy

Ingredients:

- 6 cups young arugula leaves, rinsed and dried
- 1 1/2 cups cherry tomatoes, halved
- 6 tablespoons pine nuts
- 3 tablespoons grapeseed oil or olive oil
- 1 1/2 tablespoons rice vinegar
- 3/8 teaspoon freshly ground black pepper to taste
- 6 tablespoons grated Parmesan cheese
- 3/4 teaspoon salt to taste
- 1 1/2 large avocados - peeled, pitted and sliced

Directions:

In a sizable plastic dish with a cover, incorporate arugula, cherry tomatoes, pine nut products, oil, vinegar, and Parmesan cheese. Period with salt and pepper to flavor. Cover, and wring to mix.

Separate salad onto china, and top with slices of avocado.

Nutrition (for 100g): 120 calories 12g fats 14g carbohydrates 25g protein 736mg sodium

Feta Garbanzo Bean Salad

Preparation Time : 10 minutes

Cooking Time : 0 minutes

Servings : 6

Difficulty Level : Easy

Ingredients:

- 1 1/2 cans (15 ounces) garbanzo beans
- 1 1/2 cans (2-1/4 ounces) sliced ripe olives, drained
- 1 1/2 medium tomatoes
- 6 tablespoons thinly sliced red onions
- 2 1/4 cups 1-1/2 coarsely chopped English cucumbers
- 6 tablespoons chopped fresh parsley
- 4 1/2 tablespoons olive oil
- 3/8 teaspoon salt
- 1 1/2 tablespoons lemon juice
- 3/16 teaspoon pepper
- 7 1/2 cups mixed salad greens
- 3/4 cup crumbled feta cheese

Directions:

Transfer all ingredients in a big bowl; toss to combine. Add parmesan cheese.

Nutrition (for 100g): 140 calories 16g fats 10g carbohydrates 24g protein 817mg sodium

Greek Brown and Wild Rice Bowls

Preparation Time : 15 minutes

Cooking Time : 5 minutes

Servings : 4

Difficulty Level : Easy

Ingredients:

- 2 packages (8-1/2 ounces) ready-to-serve whole grain brown and wild rice medley
- 1 medium ripe avocado, peeled and sliced
- 1 1/2 cups cherry tomatoes, halved
- 1/2 cup Greek vinaigrette, divided
- 1/2 cup crumbled feta cheese
- 1/2 cup pitted Greek olives, sliced
- minced fresh parsley, optional

Directions:

Inside a microwave-safe dish, mix the grain mix and 2 tablespoons vinaigrette. Cover and cook on high until warmed through, about 2 minutes. Divide between 2 bowls. Best with avocado, tomato vegetables, cheese, olives, leftover dressing and, if desired, parsley.

Nutrition (for 100g): 116 calories 10g fats 9g carbohydrates 26g protein 607mg sodium

Greek Dinner Salad

Preparation Time : 10 minutes

Cooking Time : 0 minutes

Servings : 4

Difficulty Level : Easy

Ingredients:

- 2 1/2 tablespoons coarsely chopped fresh parsley
- 2 tablespoons coarsely chopped fresh dill
- 2 teaspoons fresh lemon juice
- 2/3 teaspoon dried oregano
- 2 teaspoons extra virgin olive oil
- 4 cups shredded Romaine lettuce
- 2/3 cup thinly sliced red onions
- 1/2 cup crumbled feta cheese
- 2 cups diced tomatoes
- 2 teaspoons capers
- 2/3 cucumber, peeled, quartered lengthwise, and thinly sliced
- 2/3 (19-ounce) can chickpeas, drained and rinsed
- 4 (6-inch) whole wheat pitas, each cut into 8 wedges

Directions:

Combine the first 5 substances in a sizable dish; stir with a whisk. Add a member of the lettuce family and the next 6 ingredients (lettuce through chickpeas); throw well. Serve with pita wedges.

Nutrition (for 100g): 103 calories 12g fats 8g carbohydrates 36g protein 813mg sodium

Halibut with Lemon-Fennel Salad

Preparation Time : 15 minutes

Cooking Time : 5 minutes

Servings : 2

Difficulty Level : Average

Ingredients:

- 1/2 teaspoon ground coriander
- 1/4 teaspoon salt
- 1/8 teaspoon freshly ground black pepper
- 2 1/2 teaspoons extra-virgin olive oils, divided
- 1/4 teaspoon ground cumin
- 1 garlic clove, minced
- 2 (6-ounce) halibut fillets
- 1 cup fennel bulb
- 2 tablespoons thinly vertically sliced red onions
- 1 tablespoon fresh lemon juice
- 1 1/2 teaspoons chopped flat-leaf parsley
- 1/2 teaspoon fresh thyme leaves

Directions:

Combine the first 4 substances in a little dish. Combine 1/2 tsp spice mixture, 2 teaspoons oil, and garlic in a little bowl; rub garlic clove mixture evenly over fish. Heat 1 teaspoon oil in a sizable nonstick frying pan over medium-high high temperature. Add fish to pan; cook 5 minutes on each side or until the desired level of doneness.

Combine remaining 3/4 teaspoon spice mix, remaining 2 tsp oil, fennel light bulb, and remaining substances in a medium bowl, tossing well to coat. Provide salad with seafood.

Nutrition (for 100g): 110 calories 9g fats 11g carbohydrates 29g protein 558mg sodium

Herbed Greek Chicken Salad

Preparation Time : 10 minutes

Cooking Time : 10 minutes

Servings : 2

Difficulty Level : Average

Ingredients:

- 1/2 teaspoon dried oregano
- 1/4 teaspoon garlic powder
- 3/8 teaspoon black pepper, divided
- cooking spray
- 1/2-pound skinless, boneless chicken breasts, cut into 1-inch cubes
- 1/4 teaspoon salt, divided
- 1/2 cup plain fat-free yogurt
- 1 teaspoon tahini (sesame-seed paste)
- 2 1/2 tsps. fresh lemon juice
- 1/2 teaspoon bottled minced garlic
- 4 cups chopped Romaine lettuce
- 1/2 cup peeled chopped English cucumbers
- 1/2 cup grape tomatoes, halved
- 3 pitted kalamata olives, halved
- 2 tablespoons (1 ounce) crumbled feta cheese

Directions:

Combine oregano, garlic natural powder, 1/2 teaspoon pepper, and 1/4 tsp salt in a bowl. Heat a nonstick skillet over medium-high heat. Coating pan with cooking food spray. Add poultry and spice combination; sauté until poultry is done. Drizzle with 1 teaspoon juice; stir. Remove from pan.

Combine remaining 2 teaspoons juice, leftover 1/4 teaspoon sodium, remaining 1/4 tsp pepper, yogurt, tahini, and garlic in a little bowl; mix well. Combine member of the lettuce family, cucumber, tomatoes, and olives. Put 2 1/2 cups of lettuce mixture on each of 4 plates. Top each serving with 1/2 cup chicken combination and 1 teaspoon cheese. Drizzle each serving with 3 tablespoons yogurt combination

Nutrition (for 100g): 116 calories 11g fats 15g carbohydrates 28g protein 634mg sodium

Greek Couscous Salad

Preparation Time : 10 minutes

Cooking Time : 15 minutes

Servings : 10

Difficulty Level : Easy

Ingredients:

- 1 can (14-1/2 ounces) reduced-sodium chicken broth
- 1 1/2 cups 1-3/4 uncooked whole wheat couscous (about 11 ounces)
- Dressing:
- 6 1/2 tablespoons olive oil
- 1 1/4 teaspoons 1-1/2 grated lemon zest
- 3 1/2 tablespoons lemon juice
- 13/16 teaspoon adobo seasonings
- 3/16 teaspoon salt
- Salad:
- 1 2/3 cups grape tomatoes, halved
- 5/6 English cucumber, halved lengthwise and sliced
- 3/4 cup coarsely chopped fresh parsley
- 1 can (6-1/2 ounces) sliced ripe olives, drained
- 6 1/2 tablespoons crumbled feta cheese
- 3 1/3 green onions, chopped

Directions:

In a sizable saucepan, bring broth to a boil. Stir in couscous. Remove from heat; let stand, covered, until broth is absorbed, about 5 minutes. Transfer to a sizable dish; cool completely.

Beat together dressing substances. Add cucumber, tomato vegetables, parsley, olives and green onions to couscous; stir in dressing. Gently mix in cheese. Provide immediately or refrigerate and serve frosty.

Nutrition (for 100g): 114 calories 13g fats 18g carbohydrates 27g protein 811mg sodium

Denver Fried Omelet

Preparation Time : 10 minutes

Cooking Time : 30 minutes

Servings : 4

Difficulty Level : Average

Ingredients:

- 2 tablespoons butter
- 1/2 onion, minced meat
- 1/2 green pepper, minced
- 1 cup chopped cooked ham
- 8 eggs
- 1/4 cup of milk
- 1/2 cup grated cheddar cheese and ground black pepper to taste

Directions:

Preheat the oven to 200 degrees C (400 degrees F). Grease a round baking dish of 10 inches.

Melt the butter over medium heat; cook and stir onion and pepper until soft, about 5 minutes. Stir in the ham and keep cooking until everything is hot for 5 minutes.

Whip the eggs and milk in a large bowl. Stir in the mixture of cheddar cheese and ham; Season with salt and black pepper. Pour the mixture in a baking dish. Bake in the oven, about 25 minutes. Serve hot.

Nutrition (for 100g): 345 Calories 26.8g Fat 3.6g Carbohydrates 22.4g Protein 712 mg Sodium

Sausage Pan

Preparation Time : 25 minutes

Cooking Time : 60 minutes

Servings : 12

Difficulty Level : Average

Ingredients:

- 1-pound Sage Breakfast Sausage,
- 3 cups grated potatoes, drained and squeezed
- 1/4 cup melted butter,
- 12 oz soft grated Cheddar cheese
- 1/2 cup onion, grated
- 1 (16 oz) small cottage cheese container
- 6 giant eggs

Directions:

Set up the oven to 190 ° C. Grease a 9 x 13-inch square oven dish lightly.

Place the sausage in a big deep-frying pan. Bake over medium heat until smooth. Drain, crumble, and reserve.

Mix the grated potatoes and butter in the prepared baking dish. Cover the bottom and sides of the dish with the mixture. Combine in a bowl sausage, cheddar, onion, cottage cheese, and eggs. Pour over the potato mixture. Let it bake.

Allow cooling for 5 minutes before serving.

Nutrition (for 100g): 355 Calories 26.3g Fat 7.9g Carbohydrates 21.6g Protein 755mg Sodium.

Grilled Marinated Shrimp

Preparation Time : 30 minutes

Cooking Time : 60 minutes

Servings : 6

Difficulty Level : Easy

Ingredients:

- 1 cup olive oil,
- 1/4 cup chopped fresh parsley
- 1 lemon, juiced,
- 3 cloves of garlic, finely chopped
- 1 tablespoon tomato puree
- 2 teaspoons dried oregano,
- 1 teaspoon salt
- 2 tablespoons hot pepper sauce
- 1 teaspoon ground black pepper,
- 2 pounds of shrimp, peeled and stripped of tails

Directions:

Combine olive oil, parsley, lemon juice, hot sauce, garlic, tomato puree, oregano, salt, and black pepper in a bowl. Reserve a small amount to string later. Fill the large, resealable plastic bag with marinade and shrimp. Close and let it chill for 2 hours.

Preheat the grill on medium heat. Thread shrimp on skewers, poke once at the tail, and once at the head. Discard the marinade.

Lightly oil the grill. Cook the prawns for 5 minutes on each side or until they are opaque, often baste with the reserved marinade.

Nutrition (for 100g): 447 Calories 37.5g Fat 3.7g Carbohydrates 25.3g Protein 800mg Sodium

Sausage Egg Casserole

Preparation Time : 20 minutes

Cooking Time : 1 hour 10 minutes

Servings : 12

Difficulty Level : Average

Ingredients:

- 3/4-pound finely chopped pork sausage
- 1 tablespoon butter
- 4 green onions, minced meat
- 1/2 pound of fresh mushrooms
- 10 eggs, beaten
- 1 container (16 grams) low-fat cottage cheese
- 1 pound of Monterey Jack Cheese, grated
- 2 cans of a green pepper diced, drained
- 1 cup flour, 1 teaspoon baking powder
- 1/2 teaspoon salt
- 1/3 cup melted butter

Directions:

Put sausage in a deep-frying pan. Bake over medium heat until smooth. Drain and set aside. Melt the butter in a pan, cook and stir the green onions and mushrooms until they are soft.

Combine eggs, cottage cheese, Monterey Jack cheese, and peppers in a large bowl. Stir in sausages, green onions, and mushrooms. Cover and spend the night in the fridge.

Setup the oven to 175 ° C (350 ° F). Grease a 9 x 13-inch light baking dish.

Sift the flour, baking powder, and salt into a bowl. Stir in the melted butter. Incorporate flour mixture into the egg mixture. Pour into the prepared baking dish. Bake until lightly browned. Let stand for 10 minutes before serving.

Nutrition (for 100g): 408 Calories 28.7g Fat 12.4g Carbohydrates 25.2g Protein 1095mg Sodium

Baked Omelet Squares

Preparation Time : 15 minutes

Cooking Time : 30 minutes

Servings : 8

Difficulty Level : Easy

Ingredients:

- 1/4 cup butter
- 1 small onion, minced meat
- 1 1/2 cups grated cheddar cheese
- 1 can of sliced mushrooms
- 1 can slice black olives cooked ham (optional)
- sliced jalapeno peppers (optional)
- 12 eggs, scrambled eggs
- 1/2 cup of milk
- salt and pepper, to taste

Directions:

Prepare the oven to 205 ° C (400 ° F). Grease a 9 x 13-inch baking dish.

Cook the butter in a frying pan over medium heat and cook the onion until done.

Lay out the Cheddar cheese on the bottom of the prepared baking dish. Layer with mushrooms, olives, fried onion, ham, and jalapeno peppers. Stir the eggs in a bowl with milk, salt, and pepper. Pour the egg mixture over the ingredients, but do not mix.

Bake in the uncovered and preheated oven, until no more liquid flows in the middle and is light brown above. Allow to cool a little, then cut it into squares and serve.

Nutrition (for 100g): 344 Calories 27.3g Fat 7.2g Carbohydrates 17.9g Protein 1087mg Sodium

Hard-Boiled Egg

Preparation Time : 5 minutes
Cooking Time : 15 minutes
Servings : 8
Difficulty Level : Easy

Ingredients:

- 1 tablespoon of salt
- 1/4 cup distilled white vinegar
- 6 cups of water
- 8 eggs

Directions:

Place the salt, vinegar, and water in a large saucepan and bring to a boil over high heat. Stir in the eggs one by one, and be careful not to split them. Lower the heat and cook over low heat and cook for 14 minutes.

Pull out the eggs from the hot water and place them in a container filled with ice water or cold water. Cool completely, approximately 15 minutes.

Nutrition (for 100g): 72 Calories 5g Fat 0.4g Carbohydrates 6.3g Protein 947 mg Sodium

Mushrooms with a Soy Sauce Glaze

Preparation Time : 5 minutes

Cooking Time : 10 minutes

Servings : 2

Difficulty Level : Average

Ingredients:

- 2 tablespoons butter
- 1(8 ounces) package sliced white mushrooms
- 2 cloves garlic, minced
- 2 teaspoons soy sauce
- ground black pepper to taste

Directions:

Cook the butter in a frying pan over medium heat; stir in the mushrooms; cook and stir until the mushrooms are soft and released about 5 minutes. Stir in the garlic; keep cooking and stir for 1 minute. Pour the soy sauce; cook the mushrooms in the soy sauce until the liquid has evaporated, about 4 minutes.

Nutrition (for 100g): 135 Calories 11.9g Fat 5.4g Carbohydrates

Pepperoni Eggs

Preparation Time: 10 minutes

Cooking Time: 20 minutes

Servings: 2

Difficulty Level: Average

Ingredients:

- 1 cup of egg substitute
- 1 egg
- 3 green onions, minced meat
- 8 slices of pepperoni, diced
- 1/2 teaspoon of garlic powder
- 1 teaspoon melted butter
- 1/4 cup grated Romano cheese
- salt and ground black pepper to taste

Directions:

Combine the egg substitute, the egg, the green onions, the pepperoni slices, and the garlic powder in a bowl.

Cook the butter in a non-stick frying pan over low heat; Add the egg mixture, seal the pan and cook 10 to 15 minutes. Sprinkle Romano's eggs and season with salt and pepper.

Nutrition (for 100g): 266 Calories 16.2g Fat 3.7g Carbohydrates 25.3g Protein 586mg Sodium

Egg Cupcakes

Preparation Time : 15 minutes

Cooking Time : 20 minutes

Servings : 6

Difficulty Level : Average

Ingredients:

- 1 pack of bacon (12 ounces)
- 6 eggs
- 2 tablespoons of milk
- 1/4 teaspoon salt
- 1/4 teaspoon ground black pepper
- 1 c. Melted butter
- 1/4 teaspoon. Dried parsley
- 1/2 cup ham
- 1/4 cup mozzarella cheese
- 6 slices gouda

Directions:

Prepare the oven to 175 ° C (350 ° F). Cook bacon over medium heat, until it starts to brown. Dry the bacon slices with kitchen paper.

Situate the slices of bacon in the 6 cups of the non-stick muffin pan. Slice the remaining bacon and put it at the bottom of each cup.

Mix eggs, milk, butter, parsley, salt, and pepper. Add in the ham and mozzarella cheese.

Fill the cups with the egg mixture; garnish with Gouda cheese.

Bake in the preheated oven until Gouda cheese is melted and the eggs are tender about 15 minutes.

Nutrition (for 100g): 310 Calories 22.9g Fat 2.1g Carbohydrates 23.1g Protein 988mg Sodium.

Dinosaur Eggs

Preparation Time : 20 minutes

Cooking Time : 15 minutes

Servings : 4

Difficulty Level : Difficult

Ingredients:

- Mustard sauce:
- 1/4 cup coarse mustard
- 1/4 cup Greek yogurt
- 1 teaspoon garlic powder
- 1 pinch of cayenne pepper
- Eggs:
- 2 beaten eggs
- 2 cups of mashed potato flakes
- 4 boiled eggs, peeled
- 1 can (15 oz) HORMEL® Mary Kitchen® minced beef finely chopped can
- 2 liters of vegetable oil for frying

Directions:

Combine the old-fashioned mustard, Greek yogurt, garlic powder, and cayenne pepper in a small bowl until smooth.

Transfer the 2 beaten eggs in a shallow dish; place the potato flakes in a separate shallow dish.

Divide the minced meat into 4 Servings. Form salted beef around each egg until it is completely wrapped.

Soak the wrapped eggs in the beaten egg and brush with mashed potatoes until they are covered.

Fill the oil in a large saucepan and heat at 190 ° C (375 ° F).

Put 2 eggs in the hot oil and bake for 3 to 5 minutes until brown. Remove with a drop of spoon and place on a plate lined with kitchen paper. Repeat this with the remaining 2 eggs.

Cut lengthwise and serve with a mustard sauce.

Nutrition (for 100g): 784 Calories 63.2g Fat 34g Carbohydrates

Dill and Tomato Frittata

Preparation Time : 10 minutes

Cooking Time : 35 minutes

Servings : 6

Difficulty Level : Average

Ingredients:

- Pepper and salt to taste
- 1 teaspoon red pepper flakes
- 2 garlic cloves, minced
- ½ cup crumbled goat cheese – optional
- 2 tablespoon fresh chives, chopped
- 2 tablespoon fresh dill, chopped
- 4 tomatoes, diced
- 8 eggs, whisked
- 1 teaspoon coconut oil

Directions:

Grease a 9-inch round baking pan and preheat oven to 325oF.

In a large bowl, mix well all ingredients and pour into prepped pan.

Lay into the oven and bake until middle is cooked through around 30-35 minutes.

Remove from oven and garnish with more chives and dill.

Nutrition (for 100g): 149 Calories 10.28g Fat 9.93g Carbohydrates 13.26g Protein 523mg Sodium

Paleo Almond Banana Pancakes

Preparation Time : 10 minutes

Cooking Time : 10 minutes

Servings : 3

Difficulty Level : Average

Ingredients:

- ¼ cup almond flour
- ½ teaspoon ground cinnamon
- 3 eggs
- 1 banana, mashed
- 1 tablespoon almond butter
- 1 teaspoon vanilla extract
- 1 teaspoon olive oil
- Sliced banana to serve

Directions:

Whip eggs in a bowl until fluffy. In another bowl, mash the banana using a fork and add to the egg mixture. Add the vanilla, almond butter, cinnamon and almond flour. Mix into a smooth batter. Heat the olive oil in a skillet. Add one spoonful of the batter and fry them on both sides.

Keep doing these steps until you are done with all the batter.

Add some sliced banana on top before serving.

Nutrition (for 100g): 306 Calories 26g Fat 3.6g Carbohydrates 14.4g Protein 588mg Sodium

Zucchini with Egg

Preparation Time : 5 minutes

Cooking Time : 10 minutes

Servings : 2

Difficulty Level : Easy

Ingredients:

- 1 1/2 tablespoons olive oil
- 2 large zucchinis, cut into large chunks
- salt and ground black pepper to taste
- 2 large eggs
- 1 teaspoon water, or as desired

Directions:

Cook the oil in a frying pan over medium heat; sauté zucchini until soft, about 10 minutes. Season the zucchini well.

Lash the eggs using a fork in a bowl. Pour in water and beat until everything is well mixed. Pour the eggs over the zucchini; boil and stir until scrambled eggs and no more flowing, about 5 minutes. Season well the zucchini and eggs.

Nutrition (for 100g): 213 Calories 15.7g Fat 11.2g Carbohydrates 10.2g Protein 180mg Sodium

Cheesy Amish Breakfast Casserole

Preparation Time : 10 minutes

Cooking Time : 50 minutes

Servings : 12

Difficulty Level : Easy

Ingredients:

- 1-pound sliced bacon, diced,
- 1 sweet onion, minced meat
- 4 cups grated and frozen potatoes, thawed
- 9 lightly beaten eggs
- 2 cups of grated cheddar cheese
- 1 1/2 cup of cottage cheese
- 1 1/4 cups of grated Swiss cheese

Directions:

Preheat the oven to 175 ° C (350 ° F). Grease a 9 x 13-inch baking dish.

Warm up large frying pan over medium heat; cook and stir the bacon and onion until the bacon is evenly browned about 10 minutes. Drain. Stir in potatoes, eggs, cheddar cheese, cottage cheese, and Swiss cheese. Fill the mixture into a prepared baking dish.

Bake in the oven until the eggs are cooked and the cheese is melted 45 to 50 minutes. Set aside for 10 minutes before cutting and serving.

Nutrition (for 100g): 314 Calories 22.8g Fat 12.1g Carbohydrates 21.7g Protein 609mg Sodium

Salad with Roquefort Cheese

Preparation Time : 20 minutes
Cooking Time : 25 minutes
Servings : 6
Difficulty Level : Easy

Ingredients:

- 1 leaf lettuce, torn into bite-sized pieces
- 3 pears - peeled, without a core and cut into pieces
- 5 oz Roquefort cheese, crumbled
- 1/2 cup chopped green onions
- 1 avocado - peeled, seeded and diced
- 1/4 cup white sugar
- 1/2 cup pecan nuts
- 1 1/2 teaspoon white sugar
- 1/3 cup olive oil,
- 3 tablespoons red wine vinegar,
- 1 1/2 teaspoons prepared mustard,
- 1 clove of chopped garlic,
- 1/2 teaspoon ground fresh black pepper

Directions:

Incorporate 1/4 cup of sugar with the pecans in a frying pan over medium heat. Continue to stir gently until the sugar has melted with pecans. Carefully situate the nuts to wax paper. Set aside and break into pieces.

Combination for vinaigrette oil, vinegar, 1 1/2 teaspoon of sugar, mustard, chopped garlic, salt, and pepper.

In a large bowl, mix lettuce, pears, blue cheese, avocado, and green onions. Pour vinaigrette over salad, topped with pecans and serve.

Nutrition (for 100g): 426 Calories 31.6g Fat 33.1g Carbohydrates 8g Protein 654mg Sodium

Rice with Vermicelli

Preparation Time : 5 minutes

Cooking Time : 45 minutes

Servings : 6

Difficulty Level : Easy

Ingredients:

- 2 cups short-grain rice
- 3½ cups water, plus more for rinsing and soaking the rice
- ¼ cup olive oil
- 1 cup broken vermicelli pasta
- Salt

Directions:

Soak the rice under cold water until the water runs clean. Place the rice in a bowl, cover with water, and let soak for 10 minutes. Drain and set aside. Cook the olive oil in a medium pot over medium heat.

Stir in the vermicelli and cook for 2 to 3 minutes, stirring continuously, until golden.

Put the rice and cook for 1 minute, stirring, so the rice is well coated in the oil. Stir in the water and a pinch of salt and bring the liquid to a boil. Adjust heat and simmer for 20 minutes. Pull out from the heat and let rest for 10 minutes. Fluff with a fork and serve.

Nutrition (for 100g): 346 calories 9g total fat 60g carbohydrates 2g protein 0.9mg sodium

Fava Beans and Rice

Preparation Time : 10 minutes

Cooking Time : 35 minutes

Servings : 4

Difficulty Level : Easy

Ingredients:

- ¼ cup olive oil
- 4 cups fresh fava beans, shelled
- 4½ cups water, plus more for drizzling
- 2 cups basmati rice
- 1/8 teaspoon salt
- 1/8 teaspoon freshly ground black pepper
- 2 tablespoons pine nuts, toasted
- ½ cup chopped fresh garlic chives, or fresh onion chives

Directions:

Fill the sauce pan with olive oil and cook over medium heat. Add the fava beans and drizzle them with a bit of water to avoid burning or sticking. Cook for 10 minutes.

Gently stir in the rice. Add the water, salt, and pepper. Set up the heat and boil the mixture. Adjust the heat and let it simmer for 15 minutes.

Pull out from the heat and let it rest for 10 minutes before serving. Spoon onto a serving platter and sprinkle with the toasted pine nuts and chives.

Nutrition (for 100g): 587 calories 17g total fat 97g carbohydrates 2g protein 0.6mg sodium

Buttered Fava Beans

Preparation Time : 30 minutes

Cooking Time : 15 minutes

Servings : 4

Difficulty Level : Easy

Ingredients:

- ½ cup vegetable broth
- 4 pounds fava beans, shelled
- ¼ cup fresh tarragon, divided
- 1 teaspoon chopped fresh thyme
- ¼ teaspoon freshly ground black pepper
- 1/8 teaspoon salt
- 2 tablespoons butter
- 1 garlic clove, minced
- 2 tablespoons chopped fresh parsley

Directions:

Boil vegetable broth in a shallow pan over medium heat. Add the fava beans, 2 tablespoons of tarragon, the thyme, pepper, and salt. Cook until the broth is almost absorbed and the beans are tender.

Stir in the butter, garlic, and remaining 2 tablespoons of tarragon. Cook for 2 to 3 minutes. Sprinkle with the parsley and serve hot.

Nutrition (for 100g): 458 calories 9g fat 81g carbohydrates 37g protein 691mg sodium

Freekeh

Preparation Time : 10 minutes

Cooking Time : 40 minutes

Servings : 4

Difficulty Level : Easy

Ingredients:

- 4 tablespoons Ghee
- 1 onion, chopped
- 3½ cups vegetable broth
- 1 teaspoon ground allspice
- 2 cups freekeh
- 2 tablespoons pine nuts, toasted

Directions:

Melt ghee in a heavy-bottomed saucepan over medium heat. Stir in the onion and cook for about 5 minutes, stirring constantly, until the onion is golden. Pour in the vegetable broth, add the allspice, and bring to a boil. Stir in the freekeh and return the mixture to a boil. Adjust heat and simmer for 30 minutes, stir occasionally. Spoon the freekeh into a serving dish and top with the toasted pine nuts.

Nutrition (for 100g): 459 calories 18g fat 64g carbohydrates 10g protein 692mg sodium

Fried Rice Balls with Tomato Sauce

Preparation Time : 15 minutes

Cooking Time : 20 minutes

Servings : 8

Difficulty Level : Difficult

Ingredients:

- 1 cup bread crumbs
- 2 cups cooked risotto
- 2 large eggs, divided
- ¼ cup freshly grated Parmesan cheese
- 8 fresh baby mozzarella balls, or 1 (4-inch) log fresh mozzarella, cut into 8 pieces
- 2 tablespoons water
- 1 cup corn oil
- 1 cup Basic Tomato Basil Sauce, or store-bought

Directions:

Situate the bread crumbs into a small bowl and set aside. In a medium bowl, stir together the risotto, 1 egg, and the Parmesan cheese until well. Split the risotto mixture into 8 pieces. Situate them on a clean work surface and flatten each piece.

Place 1 mozzarella ball on each flattened rice disk. Close the rice around the mozzarella to form a ball. Repeat until you finish all the balls. In the same medium, now-empty bowl, whisk the remaining egg and the water. Dip each prepared risotto ball into the egg wash and roll it in the bread crumbs. Set aside.

Cook corn oil in a skillet over high heat. Gently lower the risotto balls into the hot oil and fry for 5 to 8 minutes until golden brown. Stir them, as needed, to ensure the entire surface is fried. Using a slotted spoon, put the fried balls to paper towels to drain.

Warm up the tomato sauce in a medium saucepan over medium heat for 5 minutes, stir occasionally, and serve the warm sauce alongside the rice balls.

Nutrition (for 100g): 255 calories 15g fat 16g carbohydrates 2g protein 669mg sodium

Spanish-Style Rice

Preparation Time : 10 minutes
Cooking Time : 35 minutes
Servings : 4
Difficulty Level : Average

Ingredients:

- ¼ cup olive oil
- 1 small onion, finely chopped
- 1 red bell pepper, seeded and diced
- 1½ cups white rice
- 1 teaspoon sweet paprika
- ½ teaspoon ground cumin
- ½ teaspoon ground coriander
- 1 garlic clove, minced
- 3 tablespoons tomato paste
- 3 cups vegetable broth
- 1/8 teaspoon salt

Directions:

Cook the olive oil in a large heavy-bottomed skillet over medium heat. Stir in the onion and red bell pepper. Cook for 5 minutes or until softened. Add the rice, paprika, cumin, and coriander and cook for 2 minutes, stirring often.

Add the garlic, tomato paste, vegetable broth, and salt. Stir it well and season, as needed. Allow the mixture to a boil. Lower heat and simmer for 20 minutes.

Set aside for 5 minutes before serving.

Nutrition (for 100g): 414 calories 14g fat 63g carbohydrates 2g protein 664mg sodium

Zucchini with Rice and Tzatziki

Preparation Time : 20 minutes

Cooking Time : 35 minutes

Servings : 4

Difficulty Level : Average

Ingredients:

- ¼ cup olive oil
- 1 onion, chopped
- 3 zucchinis, diced
- 1 cup vegetable broth
- ½ cup chopped fresh dill
- Salt
- Freshly ground black pepper
- 1 cup short-grain rice
- 2 tablespoons pine nuts
- 1 cup Tzatziki Sauce, Plain Yogurt, or store-bought

Directions:

Cook oil in a heavy-bottomed pot over medium heat. Stir in the onion, turn the heat to medium-low, and sauté for 5 minutes. Mix in the zucchini and cook for 2 minutes more.

Stir in the vegetable broth and dill and season with salt and pepper. Turn up heat to medium and bring the mixture to a boil.

Stir in the rice and place the mixture back to a boil. Set the heat to very low, cover the pot, and cook for 15 minutes. Pull out from the heat and set aside, for 10 minutes. Scoop the rice onto a serving platter, sprinkle with the pine nuts, and serve with tzatziki sauce.

Nutrition (for 100g): 414 calories 17g fat 57g carbohydrates 5g protein 591mg sodium

Cannellini Beans with Rosemary and Garlic Aioli

Preparation Time : 10 minutes
Cooking Time : 10 minutes
Servings : 4
Difficulty Level : Easy

Ingredients:

- 4 cups cooked cannellini beans
- 4 cups water
- ½ teaspoon salt
- 3 tablespoons olive oil
- 2 tablespoons chopped fresh rosemary
- ½ cup Garlic Aioli
- ¼ teaspoon freshly ground black pepper

Directions:

Mix the cannellini beans, water, and salt in a medium saucepan over medium heat. Bring to a boil. Cook for 5 minutes. Drain. Cook the olive oil in a skillet over medium heat.

Add the beans. Stir in the rosemary and aioli. Adjust heat to medium-low and cook, stirring, just to heat through. Season with pepper and serve.

Nutrition (for 100g): 545 calories 36g fat 42g carbohydrates 14g protein 608mg sodium

Jeweled Rice

Preparation Time : 15 minutes

Cooking Time : 30 minutes

Servings : 6

Difficulty Level : Difficult

Ingredients:

- ½ cup olive oil, divided
- 1 onion, finely chopped
- 1 garlic clove, minced
- ½ teaspoon chopped peeled fresh ginger
- 4½ cups water
- 1 teaspoon salt, divided, plus more as needed
- 1 teaspoon ground turmeric
- 2 cups basmati rice
- 1 cup fresh sweet peas
- 2 carrots, peeled and cut into ½-inch dice
- ½ cup dried cranberries
- Grated zest of 1 orange
- 1/8 teaspoon cayenne pepper
- ¼ cup slivered almonds, toasted

Directions:

Warm up ¼ cup of olive oil in a large pan. Place the onion and cook for 4 minutes. Sauté in the garlic and ginger.

Stir in the water, ¾ teaspoon of salt, and the turmeric. Bring the mixture to a boil. Put in the rice and return the mixture to a boil. Taste the broth and season with more salt, as needed. Select the heat to low, and cook for 15 minutes. Turn off the heat. Let the rice rest on the burner, covered, for 10 minutes. Meanwhile, in a medium sauté pan or skillet over medium-low heat, heat the remaining ¼ cup of olive oil. Stir in the peas and carrots. Cook for 5 minutes.

Stir in the cranberries and orange zest. Dust with the remaining salt and the cayenne. Cook for 1 to 2 minutes. Spoon the rice onto a serving platter. Top with the peas and carrots and sprinkle with the toasted almonds.

Nutrition (for 100g): 460 calories 19g fat 65g carbohydrates 4g protein 810mg sodium

Asparagus Risotto

Preparation Time : 15 minutes

Cooking Time : 30 minutes

Servings : 4

Difficulty Level : Difficult

Ingredients:

- 5 cups vegetable broth, divided
- 3 tablespoons unsalted butter, divided
- 1 tablespoon olive oil
- 1 small onion, chopped
- 1½ cups Arborio rice
- 1-pound fresh asparagus, ends trimmed, cut into 1-inch pieces, tips separated
- ¼ cup freshly grated Parmesan cheese

Directions:

Boil the vegetable broth over medium heat. Set the heat to low and simmer. Mix 2 tablespoons of butter with the olive oil. Stir in the onion and cook for 2 to 3 minutes.

Put the rice and stir with a wooden spoon while cooking for 1 minute until the grains are well covered with butter and oil.

Stir in ½ cup of warm broth. Cook and continue stirring until the broth is completely absorbed. Add the asparagus stalks and another ½ cup of broth. Cook and stir occasionally Continue adding the broth, ½ cup at a time, and cooking until it is completely absorbed upon adding the next ½ cup. Stir frequently to prevent sticking. Rice should be cooked but still firm.

Add the asparagus tips, the remaining 1 tablespoon of butter, and the Parmesan cheese. Stir vigorously to combine. Remove from the heat, top with additional Parmesan cheese, if desired, and serve immediately.

Nutrition (for 100g): 434 calories 14g fat 67g carbohydrates 6g protein 517mg sodium

www.ingramcontent.com/pod-product-compliance
Lightning Source LLC
Chambersburg PA
CBHW071816080526
44589CB00012B/811